Growth-Centered Family

A Holistic Strategy

For Better Parenting And Family Relationships

By Cecil Wong
Husband, Father, Certified LifeCoach

DEDICATION

For May, Leanne, and Randy, my forever loves.

CONTENTS

Preface: Integration

What is your life centered around? Family? Work? Play? Community? God? Whatever it is, your center sets priorities and direction, affects your choices, and most of all, profoundly impacts what and who you become. That last part is the most important thing, because of what happens to us all as we age—we, and the roles we take on, change. Our spouse changes. Our kids change. Our relationships change. Our health changes. Wouldn't it make sense to prioritize preparation for these important dynamics?

How we manage these changes either integrate or disintegrate us, and this is determined by our center, our organizing principle. How we organize and manage the various aspects of our lives shapes us. Whatever that shape is, we and our families must live with it. Hopefully, it affects those we love and live with in a positive way. Shaping occurs because whatever is central generates attention, intention, and repetition—three of the most powerful things affecting our outcomes. So, it really behooves us to focus on what deserves our best attention, intention, and repetition that give us the greatest outcome—integration. This is what will help us become the very best person we can be to lead and manage our lives and families.

Family is number one for most people, regardless of race, religion, or socioeconomics. But some things get in the way of being successful in what matters most. And what matters most is what and how we think and act. If we foster openness, courage and love, we will lead our family towards being and doing what's best. But if we permit fear to oppress and isolate us, then our kids, especially during the early formative years, will be breathing and absorbing insecurity, anxiety and worry into their souls for as long as they live with us. And who knows how they will digest and process those toxins?

When I listened to Edwin Catmull's book, *Creativity, Inc.,* I was totally stoked by the culture he and Pixar's leadership have created to uncover the hidden forces that get in the way of true inspiration. As CEO of Pixar, he with his team did this by developing structure, values, and behaviors that intentionally and effectively addressed blocks to creativity, namely unseen things that cause uncertainty and instability. For him, after achieving blockbuster success with Toy Story and Toy Story 2, his organizing principle led him to generate a company climate that encouraged his staff to be candid and open to dealing with anything that was a source of fear: people's responses and criticisms, failure, rejection, ridicule, belittling, etc. Centralizing management to tackle these emotionally charged challenges was the source of Pixar's sustainable culture of creativity. When managers willingly loosen control rather than tightening them, they're able to exercise the much needed humility and courage to become aware of what they didn't know to effectively learn and apply what was needed to achieve great outcomes.

What Ed described was the wisdom needed for effective collaboration. The environment created provided plenty of space for failure, learning, and improvement. It protected new ideas and originality (which Ed called ugly babies) from the demands of productivity (which he called the beast). This was an awesome foundation to grow a culture of excellence. Pixar has produced successful films because its leaders fostered humility and connection to consistently do things creatively, innovatively. Ed leads with head and heart working seamlessly at high levels. Smarts are obvious, but it's the priority he gives to uncovering the hidden things to optimize trust so that Pixar staff can continually discover better solutions and improve their productions. I feel this is a wonderful example for parents to follow.

Why?

Because raising children is a profound act of creation which requires high levels of creativity. Essentially, creativity is not about drawing and artistic expression. It's engagement with complex problems, of which we'll never have a shortage, and effectively seeing solutions. The best people help meet others' needs, which results in everyone moving forward to be and do their very best. The journey to seeing better is arduous and painful, but isn't this growth process exactly what we need to grow and mature? Raising kids into adults is no simple matter. Ask any stay-at-home parent about the daily dynamic challenges of balancing authority with nurturing, boundaries, and affection. Encouraging and disciplining children while also providing for basic needs requires insight across many fields of knowledge. And it is precisely this creativity that's needed to bring order out of chaos in the most important, most difficult places—our hearts, our minds, and of course, our kids. I would rank this as one of the greatest challenges we face. Just look at the endless societal problems created by dysfunctional families and delinquent youth. Whether as individuals or nations, these problems will only be overcome by leaders/parents collaboratively creating solutions at home and work to better support families raising the next generations.

Work can be central, and often is. We spend many hours of our lives working. It generally starts with elementary school and continues till we retire. Work tends to focus us on a particular subject and its parts —to learn and understand it so we can be productive and successful. And yet, oftentimes our lives become less integrated the more we work. It seems like the more productive and successful we become, the less time and attention we give to what and who we are becoming. We don't spend the time needed to grow our relationships with our spouse and kids. We don't take the time necessary time for respite and self-care. We don't invest in our personal development to improve emotionally, relationally, and spiritually. We don't commit to physical exercise to maintain or improve strength, mobility, and flexibility as we age.

As important as work is, it can be a beast when productivity drives everything. This is so common that many people don't question it. Yet, as an organizing principle, the drive for productivity has contributed to the disintegration of marriages and families. These creative acts require protection and development as the beast eats these for breakfast. The love that makes life worth living hardly stands a chance when the beast is central and calling the shots. For some, this is all they've ever known.

The concept of something else being central is entirely foreign and likely suspect; yet there are so many examples of better centers.

I have found great benefits in synthesizing subjects to grow my perspective. I see parallels across many industries and fields of knowledge and integrate them to form a holistic way of understanding life. Yeah, science and math, obviously. But how about medicine and sociology? Engineering and spirituality? Biology and belief? Leadership and parenting? Without the integration of diverse areas of knowledge, thoughts, beliefs, and protocols, we miss out on the best ways to move forward. We miss the consistent patterns of healthy, functioning, and meaningful outcomes. I've seen time and time again that life and work, presence and productivity, get better when these connections are discovered and applied to the way we live, lead, organize, and manage. And I'm not alone. Here are a few authors who express similar thoughts:

- •Chip Conley, *Peak*
- •Verne Harnish, *Scaling Up*
- •Bruce Lipton, *The Biology of Belief*

These authors draw parallels between running companies with parenting, trees, and even cellular activity. Healthy principles apply everywhere: organisms at all levels; organizations from families through corporations.

There is so much information and wisdom on leadership, transformation, parenting, spirituality, and wellness. But in my experience, the information targets narrow niches—as it should, I suppose. That's what marketing tells us to do—focus on your base. But I've found such powerful synergy when they come together! When our lives become less compartmentalized and more integrated—by a healthy soul—our interior constitution gets stronger, more manageable, more sustainable, and more of our truest and best selves show up.

An example of integration being preferred can be found in business systems. When first starting out, it's easy and common to implement disparate systems—like combining accounting software and management tools for orders, fulfillment, and customer support. But Net Suite (a cloud computing company) points out, "This tangled web of siloed business software systems…inhibits flexibility, productivity, and ultimately slows down the company's ability to grow."[1]

The same can be said for families. If there is a lack of integration, we will find ourselves less flexible and productive. This can even inhibit maturation for us and our children. Why? Because we are wired to make sense of things; 'making sense' is a big part of the first couple decades of life. And when we're living and breathing in the midst of disparate elements—i.e. life doesn't seem to have deep, substantial meaning—we can have a difficult time becoming the person we can truly be—smart, peaceful, humble, loving, skilled, joyful, benevolent. Without virtues, we will lack the creativity, courage, and sense of community to find better solutions, to take advantage of opportunities. Emptiness is the cost of disintegration.

---

[1] http://www.netsuite.com/portal/resource/articles/software-system.shtml

Because integration is so profoundly potent, our soul is the most important part of us. It's responsible for our ability to synthesize many data points, parameters, values, areas of knowledge, and experience to effectively lead and manage confounding challenges and dynamic evolutions. In this way, we generate positive, life-giving, sustainable, and even revolutionary solutions. When our soul is well, we are people of character and competence, creating healthy cultures and contributing to the redemption and revolution of the human race. How do we help our souls achieve high levels of health? We create a growth-centered family.

If this sounds ethereal, irrelevant to the real problems we face, consider the long-term view of development over a lifespan— infancy to grave. What are the real problems? Are they simple or complex? The hardest, most painful struggles are the ones no one sees, but which can damage and devastate our families. The invisible forces behind failures, rejection, loneliness, low self-esteem, and other emotional challenges often cause us to blindly subject ourselves to unhealthy routines, habits, and environments. Add to this the chronic stress and fatigue caused by sixty- to eighty-hour workweeks, and we get close to real problems. If dealing with the source of these is not part of our solution, we are living in denial, delusional of what real problems are. Without integration, we are shoveling sand against the tide.

When our souls thrive, we find solutions that make for *sustainable growth*, which becomes a central dynamic driving our priorities, strategies, and executions for what matters most—our family.

Sustainability is key. Often in business, we come across people with the mantra, "Don't do your best. Do whatever it takes." This sounds impressive, but only results in burnout, broken bodies, superficial relationships, and disintegrated souls. This is the legacy of a simplistic worldview with short-term fixes, centrally organized by work. It is unfortunately common, because a substantial long-term solution takes patience and humility in the short term; And these are unthinkable because of the hit our insecure gut and ego takes. Additionally, our interiors are fragile, disintegrated by a mindset of scarcity rather than sufficiency (more on this in Chapter 8).

We should want more, a ton more. Our core would greatly benefit with the feeling of "enough"—I have enough, I'm doing enough, I am enough. This is the root of integration. Its mantra is "Best I Can," BIC. This attitude honors the boundaries and limits necessary for health and sustainability in the most important areas—spirituality, relationships, emotion. These are the things our families need daily. Healthy constraints help us prioritize. When we don't sacrifice, but honor what matters most, life makes sense. We can live as human beings, not just human doings. With souls fully alive and thriving, we no longer sacrifice the most important for merely the important, the invaluable for the valuable, the best for the good. Chapter 9 details shifting from 'Whatever It Takes' to 'Best I Can'.

As you progress through this book, I hope you'll be excited and inspired by *your* responses to the following questions:

What does this mean for us as individuals?

What does this mean for our families?

What does this mean for our work?

What does this mean for our world?

What does this mean for our future?

I bring numerous areas of knowledge together making the precious information more accessible and connections explicit. This is not an academic, scholarly, or research-based 'treatise'. It's my personal connections of things from various aspects of life—mistakes and failures; work in faith-based ministries; work in education, both as a teacher and an administrator; postgraduate studies; volunteering and leading others; coach to parents and leaders; birthing a business; developing leadership as entrepreneur; and most importantly—my relationship with God and growing how I love my wife and kids. So, please take everything you read here as a subjective synthesis. May you find the content encouraging and helpful to your growth, your centering, and your family!

ACKNOWLEDGMENTS

My God and Savior, Jesus Christ: You are the One leading me, changing me, sustaining me to become growth-centered.

May, Leanne, and Randy, thank you for your patience and support/tolerance of my new season of growth and development.

Lisa Cerasoli (my primary editor) thank you for turning my manuscript into something readable, clarifying ideas and flow. You made the numerous rounds of improvement enlightening and enjoyable. You have a wonderful way of making constructive corrections and suggestions that encouraged me.

Doreen Meyer, thank you for your patient, perseverant proofreading that did so much to take my writing to another level of clarity. Thank you for being so thorough in getting rid of the many "will's".

Elaine Herring, thank you for your time and effort, though in the last trimester of your pregnancy, into helping my writing be less passive and more active!

Mom, thank you for your love and support of my new direction as an entrepreneur, coach, and author. After we lost dad, your ongoing growth and health are inspirational!

Growth-Centered Family

A Holistic Strategy

For Better Parenting And Family Relationships

Part One: Why center on growth?

Chapter 1: Centers

Why do some parents pressure their children toward stable jobs and focus less on pursuing passions or gifts? This pressure drives many into finance, pharmacy, medicine—careers with high-paying salaries. This 'success' may come at the cost of emotional health and maturity, creating profound challenges in marriage and parenting. In addition, risk averse career choices can derail those who don't fit into the mass mold of society. What drives this fear of instability? Protection from poverty and economic crises is a definite motivator. But there is always more than meets the eye when it comes to dealing with fear and our responses to it. Oversimplifying this issue is delusional at best and destructive at worst. It keeps us from effectively solving family problems —marital, financial, parenting. It permits the hidden roots of insecurity to perpetually plague our most precious relationships, to the disintegration of what matters most—the wellbeing of our souls, our very source of connection. We might find financial stability, and even success, but at what cost?

Being financially sound is absolutely important, but cannot be central to life. When something is central, everything else orients around it. It sets priority and direction. It shapes outcomes. It gives value, meaning, and understanding to everything else in our lives—or not. These "false centers" commonly fly under the radar. By that, I mean they cause havoc and disintegration in our lives—and yet, we never examine them; we look everywhere but at the true cause.

These centers drive financial issues, cause grief, generate substance abuse and other addictive behaviors, foster behavioral issues and academic concerns in children and adolescents, and develop mental health concerns, resulting in hostility, separation, divorce. False centers exacerbate blended family adjustments, result in chronic illness, and cause many manifestations of dysfunction. When we get stuck for long periods of time (think decades and beyond), it's likely that our center is contributing to the problem and not the solution.

Centers govern our lives. Whatever we deem most important determines our priorities. Oftentimes, we may not even be conscious about what is most important to us. We have conscious priorities, but there are also subconscious default priorities that undermine our conscious ones. Being growth-centered is about engaging these deeper core beliefs and values.

What are these instinctual centers that may be out of our purview? And if we achieve clarity about them, what will we do with them? For example, we may say that our children are everything, but at a deeper level, our decisions and goals for them can be driven by insecurity and worry rather than what will really help them thrive and succeed. It can quickly become all about what we think is best, rather than what is truly best.

I think most people would say that family is central for them, but not uncommonly, it's a notional center. Upon closer examination and evaluation, their relationships are suffering from the sabotaging effects of actual centers. Each member's development is stalled—or worse, regressing—as time, attention, and energy is given to priorities driven by deeper, instinctual beliefs and default values not centered on what makes for healthy relationships and souls.

These actual centers control how we manage our time, our behavior, and even the stories we tell ourselves. These deep beliefs determine what gives us worth and significance. It's how we deal or don't deal with the difficult emotions of shame, fear, and worry. And when these centers are left to govern for years or decades, we come to operate on defaults that may have never been consciously evaluated. We may not want them to organize our lives and our families, but we're blind to what's real, what's needed, what's best. We may even be willfully blinded, refusing to see that we are causing ourselves and others a world of hurt.

Take, for example, provision. When parents default into consistent prioritization of providing for the physiological (food and fitness) and safety (job and shelter) needs of their family members, work will become central, as that appears to be the primary source of meeting those needs. It makes sense to give more and more time and energy to our jobs: We make more money to pay for healthcare, home, education. But if time (our most precious commodity) is given to work, this equates to less time and energy with and for our loved ones. Thus, needs for love, belonging, and esteem are compromised. As a result, every family member lives with inadequately met needs for the things that truly give us worth and meaning—our connections with one another.

Whatever our center is, it cannot simply be based on the tangible; thriving, success, and fulfillment come from skill in managing the intangible, hidden things that dictate the visible. It's really about developing core values that effectively drive out fear, worry, shame, and insecurity. Perhaps the key word is "simply." We cannot expect true success from simple ways of seeing things, simple understandings, or simple solutions. The Bible gives numerous warnings against simplicity contrasting it with wisdom.

"Leave your simple ways and you will live; walk in the way of insight" Proverbs 9:6.

"The simple believe anything, but the prudent give thought to their steps" Proverbs 14:15.

"The simple inherit folly, but the prudent are crowned with knowledge" Proverbs 14:18.

"The prudent see danger and take refuge, but the simple keep going and pay the penalty" Proverbs 22:3.

All things need to be uncovered, explored, discussed, processed, evaluated, and engaged—especially simple things. Insight that can guide us toward healthy meaning, sustainable culture creation, and long-term benefits comes from a center that organizes life according to the invisible, potent things fostering faith, hope, and love. This is what I hope to share in this book, and what I hope will bring greater growth to you and your family.

Core values contribute greatly to the centers we generate. Commonly, we develop values as we grow up, based on what is impressed upon us by our family of origin and culture. These values may serve us well through school and the beginnings of our career. Hard work and sacrifice, free choice, self-determination, diversity, respect—all are beneficial. But as we enter a committed relationship with another adult and eventually start a family, these centers may need to become secondary. Why the shift? Because of what brings us together to start a family in the first place: love. Often, core values that help us succeed in education and work are not the same as those that empower us to succeed in relationships. And long-term living and loving well validates or invalidates our center.

Not all centers are equal; some are superior, some inferior. If we find ourselves giving most of our energy and time to our work (center), leaving us with only the ability to eat and sleep, our central organizing principle may be compromised. If the fruits of our labors are fulfilling and we have time for ourselves and our families, there is balance and sustainability—our center is fostering health and life-giving organization.

Get clear about what your actual center is. Decide what you really want it to be. Neglecting this will eventually produce unwanted, unavoidable outcomes in us, our health, and our relationships; our loved ones will also be affected adversely. The worst outcome is permanent disintegration, where we resign to saying, "That's just the way it is." It's okay to experience disintegration along the way, as long as we recognize it and get back on a path that restores our oneness, with God, each other, with ourselves.

Being growth-centered is not being afraid of disintegration or trying to avoid it. Rather, this way of living embraces it and redeems it through prioritizing interior life work which transforms us to become love-based rather than fear-based. Approaching life with an attitude of sufficiency rather than scarcity. Having a growth mindset versus a fixed one. Undergoing this level of change liberates us to lead and love well.

Here are three things that can help you get clear:

1. Find an online core values assessment exercise; list and rate your top five.
2. Search for a life wheel assessment to get a snapshot of how you're doing in the various segments.
3. Do an accounting of your last thirty days, identifying the amount of time you are spending on the various areas of your life.

Spend time reflecting on your findings, and figure out what is organizing it all—your center. Then, ask yourself is that what you want. If yes, great! If not, what are your options?

Choose your center wisely.

Chapter 2: Needs

We all have needs. Needs are must-haves for life; all of them. Neglecting a need is never good and results in dysfunction, decline, death, and in many cases, widespread devastation of many lives.

Abraham Maslow, a prominent psychologist of the twentieth century, studied highly healthy, successful individuals and developed a motivational theory about people. Maslow identified a hierarchy of needs that helps us see what enables us to achieve our highest potential. He began at the bottom, with physiological needs—i.e., breathing, eating, sleeping, sex, excretion. Above this was safety, that which secures health, income, personal belongings, and shelter. Then came the highly meaningful love, belonging, and esteem. When all of the lower four are met, an individual will likely be much more motivated to pursue the growth needs of cognition, aesthetics, and transcendence. Check out his pyramid at https://en.wikipedia.org/wiki/Maslow%27s_hierarchy_of_needs.

Though I don't subscribe to it unilaterally (and tend to think the distinctions between each level not so clear cut) I believe this hierarchy is helpful in understanding why we should center on growth. Maslow's model of need emergence helps us see what it takes to keep moving forward to become our best. It's a model consisting of a pyramid of five levels which are put into two primary categories: deficit (physiological, safety, love, esteem) and growth (self-actualization). Originally there were five levels. Over the years, a few more have been added—cognitive, aesthetic, self-actualization, and transcendence —to better define growth needs. Fulfilling lower-level needs gives us the support we need so higher-level needs will emerge with authentic motivation. If we want sustainable motivations to improve, we must get better and better at achieving wellness, both in the tangible and intangible realms. Trying to fulfill the higher growth levels on the pyramid (developing esteem and self-actualization) while neglecting (consciously or unconsciously) deficit needs (safety and psychological wellbeing), results in unsustainable progress.

All levels are important, but when we neglect lower ones and pursue higher ones, we end up struggling to balance, manage, and lead ourselves in the long term. The biggest struggle will be in relationships, because deficits cause us to react with instability and insecurity. With each level appropriately fulfilled, our pyramid (our soul and sense of self) will be strong. With each tier effectively supporting the ones above, we can bravely act unselfishly. Without this kind of fulfillment, lower levels cannot support the higher ones, and we lose out on the success and longevity of being all that we can be.

Fulfilling our deficit needs rather than thwarting them is an indication that our souls are well. Actually, the nature of our soul is to need. Thus, soulful living is the result of paying attention to our deficits so that our growth needs will emerge. Listening to the call of basics shapes our beliefs to value life in sustainable ways. When we care for ourselves appropriately, we will be much more able to help our family members care for themselves as well. This kind of connection liberates.

When we don't take care of ourselves, our interactions become skewed toward overprotectiveness or overt dominance—or worse, abdication and apathy. Fulfilling our needs means climbing the pyramid of growth toward being true to our best selves. This challenge requires substantial support—the support of met deficit needs. This integrates our souls with our body and our mind.

A common deficit need that gets neglected is love and belonging. These are much more difficult to fulfill than others, as they are intangible and have to do with invisible qualities and dynamics. Too often, we are overly simplistic in how we think about helping our family members feel loved and accepted. It could be that we aren't even aware of our own needs in this area. Gary Chapman offers insight here with his understanding of love languages. They are time, touch, gifts, acts of service, and words. We need each one, but generally there are one or two in particular that we gravitate toward. When we are loved with these languages, our sense of being loved is much deeper and intense. Mine are words and touch. I had my family members take the online assessment, and it was cool to see their results. Check it out: http://www.5lovelanguages.com/profile/.

Here's a list of simple definitions:
- Words of Affirmation: This language uses words to affirm, encourage, and validate the worth and beauty of your loved ones.
- Acts of Service: This language expresses care and affection through actions done for your loved ones.
- Receiving Gifts: This language is about communicating your thoughts and feelings to your loved ones through gifts that show your knowledge and understanding of them.

•Quality Time: This language is all about being present and giving your undivided attention so that your loved ones feel deeply valued.

•Physical Touch: This language expresses love and care through appropriate touch.

When love and belonging needs are met, it's likely the higher needs of self actualization will emerge. When they do, we are motivated to higher levels of creativity, morality, innovative and sustainable solutions, and openness to facts and data. With the fulfillment of unconditional love, we no longer settle for counterfeit esteem fulfillers. Unsubstantial ones will leave us wanting of the real deal, things that will authentically and healthily meet our need for self-worth. By feeling loved, we're free to find our true value. We'll be protected from shiny, blingy things that lure us with promises to make us feel significant, but actually enslaving us to fear and insecurity, resulting in blindness to what truly makes us feel valued.

I believe neglect of this area negatively shapes our brains, causing them to filter out what matters most. It leads us to operate out of fear, anxiety, apathy, or worry rather than benevolence, compassion, and courage. But effectively fulfilling this need propels us to grow into the true potential of our best selves, to be one in mind, body, and soul. Without this integration, life doesn't make sense. But with the transformative fulfillment of love, we're freed to live a life of creativity, able to make much-needed courageous moral choices, solve large-scale social problems (whether in the home or at work), and to discover and execute win-win solutions for ourselves, others, and those to come.

Just how important is it to meet each need? Is the highest as important as the lowest? What about the middle ones? I think the middle ones of love, belonging, and esteem are where we all tend to get stuck. If we don't get these met in healthy ways, we miss out on the emergence of our highest needs, i.e. to make courageous moral choices and solve large-scale problems of culture. We lose out on not being and doing what we're truly capable of, even what we were created for. Instead, we may become a cog in a massive system of exclusivity, moral decline, financial greed and corruption, and abhorrent devaluing of human life.

Meeting this middle-level need is critical to healthy fulfillment of esteem needs, which sits right above. Without a substantial sense of love and belonging for who we are, we seek to fill this need with what we do and have. The way we go about this is usually subconscious; it's no wonder why work trumps everything. When what we do becomes our organizing principle, disintegration and destruction occur.

In *Willful Blindness*, Margaret Heffernan identified many destructive, horrific tragedies in the last century caused by individuals and groups of people. Here's a partial list of those events:

- The Roman Catholic Church sexual abuse scandal in Ireland
- The Enron scandal
- The Asbestosis epidemic in Libby, Montana—one of America's worst manmade environmental disasters—and the cover up.
- The Third Reich and the Holocaust
- The 2008 Subprime Financial Crisis

• The BP Texas Fire Explosion

Heffernan observed and identified the commonalities contributing to these horrific events—conformity, competition, exhaustion, complexity, and organizational/structural opaqueness. Most, if not all, were driven by money and power. Why are these such powerful compulsions? One word: insecurity. And why so insecure? Ineffective meeting of deficit needs. I believe this is a primary cause which starts as compulsive conformity, then results in pervasive, perpetual decisions and behaviors that move one toward relational, organizational, and even societal blindness. This eventually ends with large-scale collapse and devastation of many lives.

To reiterate, why do we continue to see tragedy, hate, violence, and destruction of humanity? It's the consequence of people not healthily fulfilling their needs for love, belonging, and esteem. When the majority of our time and energy is given to our work, when our ideology is centered around soulless things, when we don't have a healthy spirituality, we will not have the motivation to prioritize; we will not commit to the long-term process of people creating sustainable cultures of trust, passion, and inspiration. The confusion and challenge of loving well, holistically thriving, finding self-worth and soul keeping is massive, regardless of where we are in the socioeconomic order, corporate-political ladder, spectrum of religions, or race. To me, it's obvious how critical the middle levels are.

But as important as deficit needs are, we can't overlook the highest-level needs of self-actualization. Sustained generational life means

17

people living successfully with objective integrity, in ways that benefit everyone, today, tomorrow, and beyond. Take, for example, trees. For trees to continually exist, they need to achieve reproductive maturity and blossom year after year. Likewise, for us, our highest-level needs must be met for positive perpetuation. In other words, the human race will continue and improve only when we have our transcendent needs met. When they aren't, we remain enslaved by fear, addictions, hostility, and dissolution.

Meeting the four foundational needs motivates us to pursue the actualization of our truest and best selves. But why do we (collectively) get stuck spending and being spent pursuing lower levels? I believe a big part of the problem here is pragmatism birthed from mindsets of scarcity. If we've always had the sense that there's never enough, that more is always better and that's the way it is, this becomes a mindset. We will consistently prioritize what is more efficient, practical, and risk averse.

Pragmatism addresses the here and now, and most often is based on what appears to be common sense. A scarcity mindset drives competition and disregard for true, sustainable wellness for all. It operates on myths created by insecurity, anxiety, and worry. It robs countless people of their potential wisdom, spirituality, courage, compassion, freedom, and transcendence, which in turn causes the deaths of exponentially more. This sounds dramatic, but history is wrought with this reality. When our highest-level needs are not being met, we devolve into the obsession with and enslavement to pursuing lower-level needs. Often, we turn them into addictions and harmful, irrational behavior rather than order and peace.

The rest of this book goes into identifying and discussing the growth it takes to break free from dysfunctional drama, whether in the deepest parts of us or those we love. Developing high levels of health at home makes our families sustainable. We bring the energy and transformation we experience into our work so that society at large can also benefit from the newness, adaptability, and innovation true love generates.

It is a grave error not to prioritize growth for meeting all needs. Through growth, we experience the emergence of our highest-level needs and their fulfilment, for others and ourselves. The growth needs of cognition, aesthetics, self-actualization, and transcendence are not merely nice to have, but rather essential to our redemption and maturation, as individuals and as a species. According to Maslow, "What a man can be, he must be." This is a deep drive. But this doesn't get prioritized when we're stuck with unfulfilled needs. They remain unfulfilled because we don't believe, at an instinctual level, that we're worth it. We live with default beliefs adopted and fostered from youth that our self-worth is based on what we do and achieve. Our esteem needs cannot be filled by achievements and possessions. They are only met by deep, proven, unconditional love and acceptance and all the accompanying behaviors of that virtue—no exceptions. If we do not experience the transformation brought about by changing environmental signals (from our living spaces, networks, inner narratives, etc.) and our perception of them, higher-level needs do not surface. Then, we miss out on what we can be—what we must be.

"The story of the human race is the story of men and women selling themselves short."

—Abraham Maslow

How common and relevant is this issue of not fulfilling highest needs? Let's just consider the most common problem that families encounter. Relational breakdowns occur between husband and wife, parents and kids, siblings with each other, and of course, the big one, parents and teens. Why do these occur? Parents prioritize and pursue career and income to provide for the lowest-level needs. While working fifty- to eighty-hour weeks, they marginalize and even sacrifice needs for belonging, love, and esteem—their kids' and their own. Attempts to make things work often fall flat because to solve their dilemmas, the parents use the same mindset/consciousness that created the problem. Albert Einstein put it this way: "The significant problems we have cannot be solved at the same level of thinking with which we created them."

Why might parents do that? Perhaps their highest needs have not surfaced because their middle needs have not truly been fulfilled. Rather than find revolutionary solutions, they operate from instincts based on outdated rules and limiting beliefs given to them as young people. These obsolete codes of the mind and heart drive them in futile pursuit of fulfillment by means that diminish their souls and the souls of those they love most. If this chain is not broken, the next generation is burdened with this stumbling block of deficiencies, inferior beliefs and rules.

In the first recorded sermon of Jesus (Matthew Chapters 5–7), He began with a need, as well—the need for spirit. Here, the Greek for spirit is *pneumati,* meaning breath, wind, or spirit. I believe this is the ultimate need—to be inspired by the Spirit, or Breath of God. It's the highest expression of our potential. It animates the transcendent acts of God and inspires our souls to do the same. ("Then the Lord God formed a man from the dust of the ground and breathed into his nostrils the breath of life, and the man became a living being" Genesis 2:7.) When this need emerges, we are living with the awareness of our continual need for His inspiration. We desire that which is sustainably beneficial and our hearts become more singular about wanting what is truly best in the long term. Our system becomes spiritually aerobic, filled with healthy emotions and relationships. We decrease the amount of time we spend doing things anaerobically without life sustaining oxygen, i.e. running the rat race. The rest of the Beatitudes expand on what it's like to live like this.

This section of the Bible describes a life deeply rooted in love, authenticity, courage, and vulnerability. Steadfastness in these qualities empowers us to pursue peace with radical conviction and commitment. Over time, substantial spirituality, justice, and compassion radiate from us. This doesn't happen through short-term fixes and efficiency. It's the outcome of a culture that wisely engages in the messiness of relationships, resulting in redemption and reconciliation. We reach this life of love through acceptance and courage in grief, pain, and tribulations. This allows us to surrender daily to what aligns most to creating and sustaining an environment of growth, grace, and revolutionary living centered on divine love that blesses and benefits all people. Often, this means forgiving others and receiving forgiveness through deep contemplation, reflection, processing, prayer, and clarity. This can be achieved through comfort-producing conversations with God, with our very own souls, with the souls of others. Regularly feeding our minds and hearts with such engagements and interactions inspires us to be spiritually aerobic. It infuses our entire bodies and souls with life.

Let's, go back to Maslow and add an essential intangible dimension to greater fulfillment—to meet needs according to spirit and inspiration. This provides higher, deeper, broader motivation. Spiritual inspiration is an inexhaustible, infinite resource for living wisely, with a perception that connects us to God, our souls, and the souls of others. It enlightens and transforms our ideologies and worldviews to align much more with the truth that we need God and His inspiration just like our bodies need air.

Centering on growth increases intention, attention, and repetition of thoughts and actions to break free from neglected essential needs. In this way, the highest needs will surface and motivate us to become what we can and what we must. In light of more recent research on Maslow's hierarchy, psychologists have produced a revised pyramid (see it at https://psychcentral.com/news/2010/08/23/updated-maslows-pyramid-of-needs/17144.html). It adds mate acquisition and retention and parenting to the top growth needs of self-actualization. I see this as an affirmation of the reality of the biblical, definitive dimension of spirituality. As creatures who reflect God's image, our primary purpose is to lovingly become one with another, cultivate a love-based, growth-centered environment, and raise another generation of people who will grow and develop greater levels of the infinite character and competence of the divine.

We center on growth so that we can get better and wiser about meeting the needs of others, as well as our own. It's a process, a journey of discovery in who we are, what life's about, and what matters most. As we grow our capacity and ability for meaning, connections, and solutions, we collectively break through barriers that limit the sustainable, responsible freedom and quality of life for all people.

Choose a center that truly fulfills needs, yours and others.

Chapter 3: Time

"Time is the indefinite continued progress of existence and events that occur in apparently irreversible succession from the past through the present to the future."[2] The fourth dimension can often be overlooked, to our downfall. Yes, time management is huge across all sectors of life and work. But often, we limit our scope to what we have to do today, tomorrow, this quarter, or this year. In other words, we focus on doing. But if we aren't factoring in *what we're becoming* and checking in to make sure we're on track as growth goes, we're missing very significant parts of the big plan. This is critical if we want to become great moms and dads. The process of becoming is the most important aspect of our lives. As long as we continue to exist and experience life, we are becoming something. The question is: what? What's happening to us as time goes on? What happens as two people fall in love, commit to each other, and start a family?

As years pass, each parent continues to evolve through their thirties, forties, and fifties. Meanwhile, babies become toddlers, school aged, adolescents, and eventually adults. Erik Erikson articulated a comprehensive theory of psychosocial development to help us understand the dynamics of growing up, from infancy through upper adulthood. Here is a chart of the progression (https://zanl13.wordpress.com/about/). Each stage has a primary crisis to be overcome, conflicts and challenges that need to be resolved (See figure.) If they are conquered, virtues are acquired.

The eight stages and potential virtues are as follows.

---

[2] https://en.wikipedia.org/wiki/Time

1.Crisis: trust vs. mistrust. Virtue: hope

1.Crisis: autonomy vs. shame and doubt. Virtue: will

2.Crisis: initiative vs. guilt. Virtue: purpose

3.Crisis: industry vs. inferiority. Virtue: competence

4.Crisis: identity vs. role confusion. Virtue: fidelity

5.Crisis: intimacy vs. isolation. Virtue: love

6.Crisis: generativity vs. stagnation. Virtue: care

7.Crisis: integrity vs. despair. Virtue: wisdom

When an individual does not succeed in a certain stage, it inhibits their movement toward greater maturity. Success involves a sense of trust in others, a healthy identity in society, and the ability to help the next generation prepare for their adult lives. One flows into the other; the latter depends on victory of the prior. These achievements are distinctly social in nature, meaning they cannot happen separate from positive, meaningful, substantial relationships.

Competing priorities—relationships, responsibilities, commitments, conflicts—complicate this journey. If home environments are dysfunctional, problems are more complex and solutions more difficult. Lack of care for our soul, body, mind, and will compromises our ability to process and connect ideas. This makes things exponentially more convoluted.

This brings us to a critical consideration if all members of the family are to thrive: are their needs being met? Deprivation or starvation doesn't contribute to success and fulfillment, and this isn't limited to the physical. From the last chapter, recall we need all levels of needs met. And, in addition to the ones that Maslow identifies, Erikson sees another dimension of needs. When all needs are effectively met, we become strong, vibrant, resilient people. Without awareness and attention to the dynamic needs that show up over time—not just physical safety and security, but the higher needs of deep, meaningful relationships, self-worth, spiritual virtues, and positive maturation—a family risks disintegration. Family dysfunction, divorce, parent alienation, and a host of other problems occur when members do not continue to grow toward healthy maturity.

Centering on growth allows us to learn to adapt, develop, and resolve the challenges of family life over the long haul. When we give substantial thought and action to time and what we become as years pass, we reduce the risk of disintegration and dysfunction. When we face stages of development aware of unseen crises and the desired virtues, we greatly increase our likelihood of a positive progression toward a life of integrity and an integrated family.

Chapter 4: The Future

Picture you and your loved ones ten to twenty years out. What's life like? What have each of you become? What choices and actions will you be making, and what will be the outcomes of those choices? What do you want your path to look like? If you don't have a clear sense of what you want to become and a conviction of what matters most, you may leave your destiny to irrelevant, perhaps even dysfunctional, defaults. Instead of being guided and empowered by wisdom and understanding, you'll simply be reactive, allowing other people's opinions (i.e. family of origin and cultural pressures) and outside circumstances to control your future.

So what's your life vision? What is your top-level, most meaningful goal? Do your daily actions line up with it? As you think about your future, what matters most is what you and your loved ones are becoming in terms of personal and interpersonal character. Those will be the biggest contributors to your fulfillment and satisfaction with life. Maturity in those areas will require continual learning and growth in your inner life and relationships.

If financial success shapes our organizing principle, making money for our families is likely our primary way of loving them. Work and home will seem disjointed and compartmentalized. We may give so much to work that we have little to nothing left for spouse and kids. When we're at home, all we can think of is work; we worry about deadlines and management issues. What is the future for this way of living? What if we could function at work and home in ways that positively benefit our coworkers and family members? Prioritizing centering on growth helps us integrate short- and long-term objectives, increasing our sense of accomplishment of heartfelt purposes.

What are your big, hairy, audacious goals (BHAGs)? The BHAG is an idea conceptualized by Jim Collins and Jerry Porras in their book, *Built to Last: Successful Habits of Visionary Companies*. The concept refers to long-term goals (ten to thirty years) that require radical personal and/or corporate change. They shift how we do things and how we're perceived by others, and even ourselves. For businesses, it could even change their industry. Collins and Porras describe BHAGs as nearly impossible to achieve without consistently working outside of your comfort zone. They involve a complete change in mindset, a passionate commitment, and bold confidence. Identifying a top level goal worthy of your conviction and commitment can profoundly change your direction and destination.

Centering on growth sets us on the path to discover and experience the transformative purposes we were created for. If we've had our lower and middle level needs effectively met, grander visions will emerge as we grow our understanding of self, awareness of the world's needs, and our calling to serve and find solutions, especially ones that bring the greatest love and joy to our families. Grand, deep, profound, meaningful plans and achievements do not usually come to us at the early stages of our lives. Sure, there are geniuses and prodigies. But for the rest of us, we need to grow to envision a plan, grow some more to execute it, and grow even more to scale it. Achieving our greatest goals requires substantial development in character and competency over a lifetime.

Lifelong relationships are essential elements of a fulfilling life. Albert Einstein achieved great things in science, but struggled and failed to keep his marriages intact. His first marriage ended after sixteen years, with his wife having an emotional breakdown from the split. He married his cousin (with whom he had started an affair sometime earlier) the same year of the divorce. He continued to see other women throughout his second marriage. I believe these difficulties detracted from greater fulfillment and potential for this awesome contributor to our understanding of the universe. Centering on growth prioritizes the wisdom needed to overcome marital and intimacy challenges to experience long-term relational success. When we elevate the importance of becoming emotionally mature, spiritually empowered, and relationally healthy, we embark on the path to overcoming the myriad of hidden challenges that come with the "goal" of sustaining lifelong love. There's so much to learn and develop in this area—healthy communication styles, peaceful conflict resolution, hope-giving emotional hygiene. We will address much of this in section three, Cultivating a Growth-Centered Family.

Parenting is a huge part of a desired life vision. Every mom and dad wants to do well in this awesome role. No one wants to be a bad parent, but unfortunately, failed strategies are common. Most, if not all, of our most challenging problems can be attributed to ineffective parenting tactics and ideologies. Successfully raising kids requires strong parental relationships. For many parents, healthy relationship practices get neglected. And without this source of trust and love, we end up resorting to inferior substitutes.

Why do we do this? Non-growth centers will inhibit learning and positive changes. Centers normally operate from our subconscious. If we've never investigated and evaluated the subsurface parts of us, it's likely our parenting lacks liberating elements. Instead, we're probably engaging our kids with limiting, outdated beliefs and rules. It's tough, if not impossible, to succeed as moms and dads if we carry around unhealthy expectations and controlling patterns and habits. This can indicate a lack of healthy growth through the stages of autonomy and initiative. When this cycle remains unbroken, we end up simply reacting (ineffectively) to stress and tensions with blind over scheduling, explosive ruptures that don't get repaired. Over time, our family health and vitality diminishes.

If you have a vision for a happy, thriving family, you need to grow. As time passes, consistent behaviors will have compounding effects— for good or bad. Watch out for chronic, negative developments— distrustful behaviors, disrespect, dysfunction. These are signs of need to grow in leadership. You need a core of honesty, courage, and compassion—first with yourself, then with others. These values foster positive, humble, intimate knowledge of self that results in effective self-direction. It's this authenticity driving actions to pursue life-giving, effective solutions for family problems—solutions that free and empower each family member to thrive. You can think of self-knowledge as headlights that light up the road ahead. Without it, you might do okay during the day, but when night falls, your ability to see and navigate is compromised.

Without vision, your goals may actually prove detrimental to your family's health. The most positive and significant goals in life promote freedom. Freedom is the central purpose of growth. Freedom from the enslavement of chronic problems that decrease and diminish our lives, whether poverty, relational breakdown, or disease. Being growth-centered is being a freedom fighter against chronic stress, atrophying environments, negative effects of aging, debilitating effects of loss and trauma, and a host of other challenges to your family's well-being.

Growth in what matters most inspires and empowers us to envision and achieve BHAG's with those most precious to us. Being growth-centered keeps us open to deepening our understanding, broadening our scope, and elevating our purpose for a grander vision. This is the divine design for us to become who and what we really are—lifelong lovers that birth and raise a new generation that will perpetuate and even expand true love to redeem and transform society. When we stop growing, we actually derail ourselves from the path of real life and miss out on being a part of God's renewal process. Look inside any family or organization that is growing and you will find an organizing principle that cultivates long-term maturation, in those leading as well as those being led. As our family sees our progress and transformation, they will be inspired and open to our leading, and encouraged to do the same.

Greater vision and big, hairy, audacious goals invariably involve scaling up. A growth center prioritizes preconditions for scaling up by optimizing connections. Much like the roots of a tree, such a center maximizes the surface area it reaches and connects and bonds with the soil that gives it life. Centering on growth compels us to create environments of substantial connection to maximize space and time for activities needed to learn and change. One great example is carving out regular time for rest. We have to respect the limits of our bodies and minds—master the restlessness by surrendering to peace, working against defaults driving us to exhaustion and disintegration. Prioritizing time to bond and enjoy each other consistently fortifies trust, strengthening our trajectory toward a desired vision. We become better managers of the core values organizing or disorganizing our lives and work.

Without this growth, we miss out on greater productivity, innovation, and sustainability—healthy goals of scaling up. An environment consisting of a balance of rest, sufficiency, genuine love, trust, courage, and belief in self and others is an environment that frees us, creating greater productivity, engagement, innovation. This is sustainable. Kids need such a center to grow their autonomy and initiative. It's what adolescents need to appropriately transform their identity from kid to adult. This environment feeds intimacy between couples. It empowers us to positively impact the world and profoundly shape a unified perception of our life story—with all the pain and pleasures, failures and successes, love and fear, brokenness and wholeness.

Non-growth centers keep us bound to the past, rather than allow us to learn and make corrections. We are closed to current data, change, and evolution—we do not adapt to think and act significantly or relevantly. Most important, we don't act lovingly to liberate and empower ourselves and others toward greater success and fulfillment.

Our future depends on how we perceive reality, respond internally, and act on our resolves. Our best future is calling us to fulfill our purpose and be part of God's unfolding plan of freedom and redemption for everyone. Our worldview is an essential, critical part in this story. Considering the vastness of the universe, with all its complexity and the incredible profoundness of life, pain, and love, it's foolish to stop growing, to not amass wisdom for this journey. Not only is it foolish, it's detrimental—human history is littered with the decline and devastation of those who centered on lower-level needs rather than what would effectively meet those and move people onward. What stopped them from progressing in the way of trust, love, and freedom? I propose a stunted worldview shaped by fear and insecurity. Souls diminished and disconnected from those of others because of environments where relationships were not challenged and supported, but fueled by unhealthy management of stress and painful emotions. Relationships and emotions go together like a hand goes into a glove. Part Three of this book will focus on the cultivation of these two areas that radically determine our openness to growth, change, and development.

Chapter 5: Challenges

Having vision and BHAGs is awesome, but then comes the arduous process of achieving them. There will be challenges, the kind that will knock you down many times, possibly even knock you out. Success will require profound wisdom and unbelievable grit. Why center on growth? To increase our knowledge, understanding, mindset, strength, strategy, execution, evaluation, and repetition so that we can achieve the big, hairy, audacious goals we're made for.

In this chapter, we'll look at four of what I feel are the most significant challenges to having a sustainedly happy, healthy, thriving family:

1. **Marriage**, the union of two that creates the home environment

2. **Parenting**, the foundation for the children's development

3. **Health and fitness**, contributing much to the general sustained wellbeing of each family member through the stages of development

4. **Dysfunctional culture elements** and their influences, external and internal

Overcoming these four challenges will require substantial growth in who we are and what we do—growth that will redefine how we view life, our loved ones, and even what life is about.

Marriage

Marriage can be both amazing and transformative yet awful and ass-kicking (it knocks us down and possibly out). Here's a laundry list of what makes marriage so difficult:

●Communication breakdown—i.e., blame, criticism, stonewalling, aggression, the silent treatment. Basically, a lack of clear, meaningful dialogue from the heart.

Conflicts are like a slippery slope. When we are on opposite sides, it's easy to slide off the top of the slope into avoidance and/or aggression that dwell at the bottom. We either shut down or we attack. Whichever way we go, it's generally caused by unhealthy management of fear. This causes the breakdown of trust and honesty, eroding the intimacy we've cultivated with our loved ones. Our marriages need to be supported with robust intrapersonal character that passionately protects intimacy. Our hearts' desire to thrive in the long-term is what makes our marriage last. Marital disintegration, however, will follow these:

1. Emotional immaturity, due to consistent neglect of addressing feelings as they arise.
2. Ongoing stress, created by imbalance of work, play, rest, and time spent with loved ones.
3. The absence or reduction of physical intimacy (sex), due to the previous two factors.
4. Resentment, due to the previous three factors.

Those are four really good reasons to center on growth. If you go into marriage with no awareness of the above or an unwillingness to deal with their challenges, you'll be quickly thrust into the crucible of a dysfunctional relationship.

Maybe you do have a heads up on those difficulties. In this case, you may want to consider evaluating your mindset and tools. Do you see yourself heading into a friendly sparring bout or a professional MMA competition? Are you going into a gunfight with a knife? Will you be playing a board game, or will you be fighting for your life?

Marriage is no walk in the park. It's a super marathon. It's not about control but courage. It's not just providing and pleasing, but being patient and leading, proving "your love is real." It's doing whatever it takes to eliminate threats to the trust and wellness of your relationships. It's about commitment to your loved one.

What will you do to survive the storms of marital challenges and their weathering effects? Grow wisdom and grit. I suggest developing a growth-centered family.

Parenting

Another challenge to success and fulfillment as a family is parenting with unhealthy centers and failed strategies. This challenge has numerous elements: unhealthy expectations, controlling patterns/habits, ineffective ways of handling disrespect and attitude, poor conflict resolution, overscheduling of extracurriculars, and lack of clear, meaningful dialogues. And these are just the tip of the iceberg.

Expectations

So many expectations are impressed upon us from youth that if we haven't gone through the process of filtering, evaluating, and reassembling life's meaning for ourselves, we're going to have way too many expectations for our kids (and ourselves, too). These expectations cloud our view of what matters most, creating unhappy environments—kind of like cold, cloudy weather prevents sunshine from lighting and warming life.

Addiction to Control

The habit of, or addiction to, control inhibits vision and achieving BHAG's. As people develop from infants into adults, they need space and freedom to develop. What they don't need is static, anxiety-based, performance-driven control. If we find ourselves stuck with a compulsion to micromanage, it's likely we have unaddressed needs or even wounds draining us of energy for change and growth. Our worldviews are limited and outdated. We aren't keeping up with what's going on with our family members. We're out of touch with our own lack of development and maturity in the things that matter most to thriving family.

Managing Disrespect

Underdeveloped inner lives generally have a hard time with disrespectful attitudes and behaviors. Ruptures occur and without the discipline and exercise of patience, reflection, intimate examination, and dialogue, we tend to react mindlessly without intention for healthy resolve and repair. We slip into either silence or violence. Neither contributes to effective parenting to lead our kids toward growing up to be smart, loving, and brave. If anything, it just elevates their fight/flight responses, which will perpetuate their undesired responses and perceptions.

Poor Conflict Resolution

This one comes back to bite us when we haven't worked it out in our marriage. Conflict will occur with our children, and it should— conflict management and resolution is an essential life skill.

Our kids will not go along with every limit we set. We also will not and cannot give into all of our kids' requests and wants. And presto, conflict! Will these moments become patterns of slipping and reactivity?

Or will they help each person become a thoughtful and sincere resolver who grows the relationship with greater trust, honesty, and commitment?

If we're consistently silent, we become less and less honest, and the other is permitted to continue to think and act without clarity and challenge. If we're explosive, inflammatory, and accusatory, we'll likely shut down honesty and trust and go on operating on inferior, unchallenged ideas. No one wins when our fight/flight responses are in control. Needs aren't being met, psychosocial stages aren't being successfully navigated, and leadership isn't being developed.

Over-scheduling

To further challenge health and happiness in our homes, we over schedule our kids and ourselves so we don't have enough PDF[3] (play, down, family time). This is unstructured time for play, rest, and bonding, which are essential for envisioning, reflection, restoration and renewal from stress hormones, and strengthening connections between parents and siblings. This is especially critical during adolescence, when kids are transforming into adults—much like the caterpillar liquefying in a cocoon to reorganize itself into a beautiful butterfly.

---

[3] http://www.challengesuccess.org/parents/parenting-guidelines/

Stanford University's education department's mantra is "Challenge Success." They've done research and development to help parents and schools find alternate modes and methods for success. Over the last several decades, they've not only recognized the harm in over-scheduling, they've identified and promoted the need for PDF. Just tolerating minimal amounts is not enough; large chunks of this time are vital. They've found this is key not only to academic success, but to real, sustainable success and fulfillment in work and home life.

Over-scheduling drains teens of time and energy for transformation and individuation. It shouldn't surprise us that so many adults continue to think and act immaturely, without a deep sense of who they are, unable to deeply know and be known by one another. They get a job and run the rat race, unaware of how to generate life-giving relationships with their precious loved ones. Then they find themselves in the latter half of life, unable to make real, meaningful sense of their lives. Moreover, they do not become the thriving life managers they could have been if they had let go of the old and generated a newness unique to themselves.

Something to get clear about—what drives it all? Is it fear of missing out or being left behind? Is it coming from a scarcity mindset based on negative experiences and emotions—the stuff we tell ourselves we don't have time for, or question sarcastically. All these do is perpetuate attitudes and behaviors keeping us stuck in unhealthy ways of relating to our loved ones. If our kids get caught up in this dysfunction, their healthy independence may be challenged or compromised.

When it comes to our schedules, less is more. A slower pace creates time and space for making meaning, lowering stress hormones in our blood, and setting a trajectory toward healthy maturation. This progress leads to healthy independence. If we're not used to this, it will be uncomfortable initially. But it's worth it if we're willing to deal with difficult, unseen things to make sense of deeper issues we avoid or don't see. Slow down to go farther, stronger, longer. This is the only way to discover and achieve the most important long-term goals, benefiting everyone. It's the road to win-win solutions that do not come to us when we're overbooked, overstressed, and overcome by the beast of productivity.

Clear, Meaningful Dialogues

This leads us to a root of these challenges—a lack of clear, meaningful dialogues. Without these conversations, we don't understand each other in ways that foster positive changes in attitudes and actions. If we are to move forward toward the grand vision and BHAG of a dynamic, thriving family, we need to have these talks. We also have to get better at these talks. To be our best, we and our loved ones must experience healthy expression and exchange of love and freedom on a consistent basis.

When these conversations are missing, we are left to our own presuppositions, assumptions, and interpretations of what we see and hear. Have these internal thought elements matured to provide us the courage and compassion to connect meaningfully, constructively, and most importantly empathetically during conflicts, especially with those we love most?

When our interior capacities and mechanisms have not been evaluated and worked on, we default into avoidance or aggression if stakes are high and chips are down. We're flying blind with faulty instruments. Without health in this area, our relationships go awry, then crash and burn.

If we do the necessary work to improve our underlying beliefs, values, and processes, we master the stories we tell ourselves. Mastery gives us the ability to stay present in a conflict, to listen, engage, and share meaningfully and appropriately to foster encouragement and openness. Empowering these behaviors is a story generating positive emotions, sustaining and strengthening our bonds with the other. Simultaneously, we gain mutual understanding of each other's points of view.

Obtaining deeper, mutual understanding is a key skill of healthy leadership and crucial for parenting and marriage. Difficult dialogues come from deep resolves about what matters most; they develop our perspectives to honor everyone's thoughts and feelings. No one needs to feel ignored, shut down, or dominated. Both people can be honest and heard. These conversations both require and foster growth as we engage one another.

More about cultivating inner life clarity and fortitude to grow our ability to have meaningful dialogues in Part Three.

<u>Health & Fitness</u>

Another common obstacle to our vision and goals is a lack of health and fitness. Sure, getting sick happens, and we can't avoid all injuries and accidents. But without routines to improve our wellbeing, strengthen our resistance to disease, increase our strength and resilience, attacks and mishaps will be more frequent. They will increasingly impede our time and ability to move toward our goals and desired life destinations. In other words, we need sound strategies to positively manage the effects of aging. What will we be like when our kids are adolescents? When they're young adults? When they become parents and we become grandparents?

Let's start with stress. Some stress is good; it can increase strength and sharpen our skills. But consistent exposure of our mind and body to chronic, high levels substantially compromises our longevity. In an article in Helpguide.org, Segal, Smith, Segal, and Robinson put it this way: "…beyond a certain point, stress stops being helpful and starts causing major damage to your health, your mood, your productivity, your relationships, and your quality of life… Chronic stress disrupts nearly every system in your body. It can shut down your immune system, upset your digestive and reproductive systems, raise blood pressure, increase the risk of heart attack and stroke, speed up the aging process and leave you vulnerable to many mental and physical health problems."[4]

A lifestyle pervaded by stress will likely lead to extremes of activity or inactivity. This, in turn, leaves us ill-prepared for the effects of aging, accidents, traumas, losses, and diseases. It is essential to create and sustain dynamic balance in our lives improving our overall health and fitness. Then, we can be there for our loved ones, contribute significantly to the world, and continue to live freely, joyfully into our upper years, and realize our highest potentials.

Being growth-centered helps us identify changes and opportunities for greater health and fitness even as we age. My mother is a great example of this, as she is stronger as a seventy-nine-year-old than she was twenty years ago. In the last twenty-five years, she's become a vegetarian, a regular on the tennis court (almost daily), and a gym rat (three or four times a week). We enjoy weekly gatherings with her, and rather than worry about her, we're consistently amazed at her vitality and strength.

Dysfunctional Cultural Elements

---

[4] https://www.helpguide.org/articles/stress/stress-symptoms-causes-and-effects.htm, Jeanne Segal, Ph.D., Melinda Smith, M.A., Robert Segal, M.A., and Lawrence Robinson.

This last challenge is a big one, and anytime you consider the wider context, things get a lot more complex and confounding. On *Inside Quest with Tom Bilyeu*[5], *Simon Sinek* identified four cultural factors that are challenging millennials (those born 1984 and after) in meaningful job satisfaction and relationship fulfillment. I find his insights helpful in developing greater parenting strategies and skills. The factors are:

1. Failed parenting strategies that fostered low self-esteem

2. Too many celebrations for no real achievements

3. Lack of substantial challenges

4. An overabundance of fluffy support; enablement—entitlement being the result.

Outside the family dynamic, societal trends effect us:

- Emotional Immaturity because technology has enabled this generation to put up filters, giving others the impression that their lives are awesome (using "likes" to boost low self-esteem).

- Impatience (another offshoot of technology)—immediate gratification through technology is a big issue for millennials.

- Emphasis on bravado, due to corporate environments prioritizing productivity and performance over personal development—work places lacking healthy leadership and strong values to create long-term success for all suffer from this performance over personal development.

---

[5] Episode of Inside Quest, Dec 28, 2016, https://www.youtube.com/watch?v=5MC2X-LRbkE

I sum these up as a lack of sustainable leadership to grow and develop character, to overcome dysfunctional cultures and to thrive in new, adaptive, and even revolutionary ways. Most, if not all dysfunction is the result of conformity caused by centering on things other than growth. Centers driven by fear-based responses to challenges perpetuate stress. At a deeper level are outdated rules and limiting beliefs from ineffective processing and interpretation of the world.

At the root of this challenge is the need for patience—slowing down enough to find balance and build trust. Balance and trust are keystones to job fulfillment, self-confidence, and significant impact. All of that takes time. If you're impatient, you will not take the time to discover meaningful priorities and create balance; you will not create and protect the time it takes to truly bond and make good on your promises and commitments to those who mean the world to you. Just look at the lives of those who are in a rush—rush to find a partner, rush to make a fortune, rush to climb the corporate ladder, rush to show their competence and prove themselves. What happens to their family relationships? Disintegration is not an uncommon outcome.

Without the patience to develop balance and grow trust, we will likely devolve into silos, sacred cows, lack sustainable leadership and exhibiting distrustful behaviors and patterns. Perhaps the most significant downfall will be the lack of clear, meaningful dialogues to figure out what's wrong and to course correct.

The challenges discussed in this chapter are profound and require a different way of thinking and doing. We need new approaches coming from a different consciousness. Obstacles to wellness, success, and significant contribution exist when we center on things other than growth. They get us stuck, and if we don't respond with courage and openness to change (growth), we will not discover where the problem truly lies, how to find answers, and who can help us develop the mindset for real solutions.

Part One Summary

Most of our challenges find their source in unmet needs. We struggle in marriage and parenting because unmet needs (love, belonging, esteem) drive behaviors that break down trust and communication. To add to this, our health may be compromised due to unmet physiological needs caused by neglect of self and soul driven by unmet esteem needs, buoyed by unmet love and belonging needs. It's a self-defeating cycle.

When we lack vision for what we are created to become—adults capable of intimacy, generativity, and integrity—we default and succumb to common dysfunctional cultural values and outdated expectations from our family of origin. We let the simpler solution of work define us. We become bankers, lawyers, doctors, engineers, political leaders, business executives, and employees supporting the beast-like machines of our economies, rather than becoming the lovers, spouses, parents, and servant leaders our precious ones need us to be.

When we do not center on our growth as people in families, we devolve into willfully blind individuals and societies living and dying by failed marriages, parenting strategies, compromised health, and dysfunctional cultures. We are impotent to meet or provide opportunities for true success and the fulfillment of our best selves—loving souls.

But what happens when we organize around the things that support growth—fulfilling all levels of needs, moving forward in our psychosocial development, improving our leadership and management of our inner life consciousness? Transformation. Transformation of who we are, what we do, and how we do life. And from this deep change, we become part of God's redemptive work, which is the only thing that will make sense of the human story, our stories, our lives—us. We make sense when we think and act with a vision for growth that integrates all we are and do to create a liberating story of love and redemption.

Part Two: What is a growth-centered family?

Introduction: A Strategy

In light of the why's in Part One, what will a family look like when centered on growth? That's what I hope to describe in this section. The big picture of needs, stages of development, future goals, and challenges help us see the highly significant and fundamental purpose for what I'm sharing. A growth-centered family aligns with the universe by optimizing relationships, fulfilling souls, and embracing transformation as the way to become liberated leaders. Parenting this way empowers us to raise our kids with dynamic relationships that challenge and support them appropriately according to their changing needs.

This is a long-term strategy for success and fulfillment: make sure we're getting needs met—others' and our own—and work at getting better at it. Be mindful about where we and our loved ones are at in life; this helps us understand their needs and which ones to prioritize. Have a vision for authentic, dynamic, heart-focused leadership. We've got to have a destination and direction that inspires us to be and do what we were made for.

This strategy creates an environment that develops a perception of love and liberty. This creation includes both internal and external landscaping. It's about cultivation of habits, beliefs, and values that, if firmly planted in our lives, will produce desirable fruit. This means we'll need to take on the role of a gardener. We can actually see this at the beginning of the Bible, and I'd like to take a look at this reference and the immediate context:

"The Lord God took the man and put him in the Garden of Eden to work it and take care of it" Genesis 2:15.

The Creator's primary, fundamental purpose for man is cultivation of his environment to generate and sustain life for all. And in this environment, man was given access and even direction to eat from any and all trees except one. This tree was a source of confusion—knowing good and evil.

"And the Lord God commanded the man, 'You are free to eat from any tree in the garden; but you must not eat from the tree of the knowledge of good and evil, for when you eat from it you will certainly die'" Genesis 2:16, 17.

And the confusion would be a malignant one causing harm, injury, disease, and pain. Further on in the narrative (Genesis 3), we see the fruit of disobeying the prohibition was shame and death. The man and woman hid from God, became mortal, and had a son who eventually killed his younger brother.

Immediately following that instruction and warning came the intention for a helper, a soulmate.

"The Lord God said, "'It is not good for the man to be alone. I will make a helper suitable for him'" Genesis 2:18.

Thus, cultivation and care of life would not be a lone venture, but rather one done intimately with another. This is the ordained design of the family, the primary way for human beings to generate sustainable life—a man and a woman becoming one to create and cultivate an environment in which new life can thrive and learn to care for one another and the world outside the family circle.

What are you cultivating in your home? In your heart? In your relationships? Cultivation takes time, intention, and repetition. Values need to be planted and watered. What they're planted in needs to have nutrient qualities, just like good soil. Location matters, too. This may seem obvious, but the seed planted also needs the capacity to grow and produce life. What are these qualities?

Belief, trust, courage, benevolence, to name a few. How do we cultivate these? Well, they are intangible, invisible. This means we need to grow our knowledge and understanding into the unseen, hidden things—the stuff and forces inside our minds, hearts, and souls. Part Three will delve into these areas, encouraging you to prioritize and commit to their growth. Then, you will have greater wisdom to help your family thrive and achieve long-term wellness, fulfillment, and success in all things.

As a gardener, cultivating activities involve caring for your own soul as well as relationships with your loved ones. Chapters 11 will focus on your interior life, and chapter 12 and the appendix will present skills and tools for growing clarity and communication from numerous sources (noted in the bibliography). As you develop your practice, it's my hope that you will experience more joy, strength, and true love.

The "why's" in Part One provide a context to understand our roles as parents with strong implications for leadership. The growth-centered strategy addresses the top priorities that the big picture reveals. Commitment to this blueprint helps us develop true love, freedom, and wisdom—what we all need to better lead and serve those we love and beyond.

Chapter 6: Aligned with the Universe

A growth-centered family is a unit of people living in accordance with the most important, unchanging principles of the universe.

There is order in this world, and thanks to many areas of knowledge, we're learning more about it now than ever. For us humans, there are two mega-categories in which we would do well to develop a high level of understanding and application: *time* and *life*. More specifically it's what life does as time passes. How we perceive and deal with life and its changes (ours and others') is at the root of what determines our movements, conditions, resiliencies, and destinations. Our family's quality of life, direction, success, and fulfillment can be traced to how we understand its purposes, evolutions, and stages from beginning to end. When we align with the created order, centering on what matters most, we can continue to grow in vitality, freedom, grace, and gratitude.

Time

I call time a dynamic constant. It's always around, but it never stays put. Moreover, its effects are comprehensive because of the many factors and forces existing and occurring as time passes. This means change is also a dynamic constant. Weather is a great example of what I'm talking about. Consider its elements: temperature, humidity, precipitation, wind, UV rays. They exist 24/7 and continually affect everything exposed to them, changing appearances, breaking things down, etc. If we want to have a home that will hold up under all weather conditions, we will need the materials and design to withstand wind, rain, sun, and snow.

Atmospheric conditions have a parallel in the area of human interactions. Relationships create climates and weather of sorts. And just as physical weather and climates affect everything within their regions, our relationships affect everything about us and those we're connected to. Collectively, our relationships and their effects make family life quite complex. And just as with the homebuilding example above, for our families to weather the various challenges of life, we need to build with quality materials and proven designs.

There are three universal elements that we need to get clear about to fortify our families against the weathering effects of time.
- Communication Complexities
- Aging
- Being Alive

Communication Complexities

Living with loved ones is awesome, but it can be just as difficult as joyful. Challenge and complexity are compounded the closer we are with another person, and continue to compound as the number of these close relationships increases. When it's two of you, there are two channels of communication, two degrees of complexity. And you know how difficult this can be. Becoming one with another is magical and mysterious, highly challenging to make last, even more to last well. Why? Well, here's a brief list of what communication can involve:

- Listening
- Candor
- Respect
- Humility
- Self-esteem
- Trust
- Forgiveness
- Hurt
- Failure
- Empathy
- Emotion
- Courage
- Stress
- Fear
- Compassion
- Trauma
- Loss
- Loneliness
- Guilt
- I'm sure you can add more!

When you add one and become three, your family has grown 50%, but communication channels increase to six, a 300% growth in complexity. Add a fourth, and complexity quadruples to twenty-four channels. That's 33% growth in size, but 400% in complexity. When you had your second kid, did you realize the complexity of your family would spike exponentially? With child #3, forty lines of communication —you can do the math.

Are you aligned with this complexity growth? If we're misaligned, our homes will likely be filled with tension and strife—shouting matches, manipulation, uncontrollable meltdowns, lots of useless nagging, eye rolling, caustic sarcasm, all resulting in relationships breaking down from a lack of healthy, effective communication.

Our personal growth is a must for effective responses to "evolutions and revolutions" of our family. When we grow, we improve our ability to revolutionize the world of our relationships by how we communicate, how we love and care, how we lead and serve… dynamically over time.

Aging

The evolutions from infancy to adolescence bring many changes and challenges—personalities emerging, individual uniqueness and interests, conflicts at home and school, joys and sorrows, pains and pleasures, awesome ups, devastating downs, crises, celebrations, along with all the physical, mental, emotional, and spiritual changes that come with increasing development. The same can be said for progress from young adulthood to upper adulthood. Manifestations of change vary; nevertheless, change is always dynamic and difficult.

However, when we center on growth, we align with the dynamics of time, complexity, and changes to learn and effectively respond to evolutions and crises. Growing our understanding into each life stage enlightens us to generate revolutions of greater joy, love, wisdom, fulfillment, and commitment.

When we are clear about where we're at and we're going in terms of psychosocial development, we make wiser choices about the beliefs and rules we want to embrace and apply to ourselves and our families. We will be much more able to help our loved ones be and do what they were created for. We bring out the best in them rather than focus on what we've been told by those who know neither our family members nor the relevant context in which we live. Moreover, those who try to tell us they know better likely have not experienced significant liberation from the antiquated code of their past. If they had, they would not have the "I know better" attitude; rather, they'd recognize the potentials and opportunities when people are open to learning, adapting, creating, and maintaining new disciplines. And all this is possible because of healthy relationships driving out fear and anxiety, keeping the mind and heart open.

To illustrate, consider the growth of an individual. Beginning with infancy, he is fully dependent for practically everything. But in a short time, somewhere between the longest days and the shortest years, he becomes mobile and verbal. From toddlerhood to grade school, habits, and patterns shape relationships and a culture emerges. Will the created environment support the volatility of adolescence? What kind of communication will have developed? Avoidance? Aggression? Passive aggressiveness? Manipulation? Siloed operations? It's okay to have moments of these. They're not to be avoided; rather, we want to see them as opportunities for meaningful change. The need is to develop revolutions in the midst of our children's evolutions—new ways of leading and managing as they grow in capacities and capabilities. Some parents struggle and successfully make these transitions. Sadly, some never do.

We can't relate to our kids the same when they're toddlers as when they're infants. We can't give our kindergarteners the choices we give our adolescents. Many parents do not provide age-appropriate, supportive structures and disciplinary actions to help their children make good choices. They simply use words, futilely hoping that things will improve. The repeated decision to do the same thing over and over can result in the blindness that enables youth to get steeped in bad choices, destroying their own lives and probably causing harm to others.

It's consequences that really teach. In real life, mistakes have tangible consequences, not just words. Without consequences, our children will continue to make wrong choices, not learn the right ones. This will result in a number of negative outcomes—low self-esteem, lack of respect for others, and many other dysfunctional, devastating patterns. But in order to effectively learn from consequences, there must be an environment of healthy relationships.

"Rules without relationship leads to rebellion." Author-speaker Josh McDowell has taught this principle for decades. When parents struggle to effectively discipline their children, especially as they get older, it's because their relationship with them needs improvement and development, maybe even healing. The environment of connections either opens the mind and heart to receive and give (receive instruction, correction; give trust, respect), to close up and reject, or a convoluted mixture of the two. (More on this in the next chapter.)

Why do some parents continue in futility? They haven't aligned with the universal, dynamic constant of time. They haven't become mature communicators who are courageously and compassionately gaining mastery over their interior landscape. They aren't able to express their thoughts and feelings honestly and respectfully. If they could align with time, they would develop the desire and ability to empathetically understand others as they understand themselves.

Aligning with time is being aware of each stage of psychosocial development for ourselves and each member of our family, prioritizing what is most important to successfully navigate through them. This is something we do not want to oversimplify or overcomplicate. What we do need to do is identify priorities. Consistently implementing them will both challenge and support us and our loved ones to greater ownership and wiser choices when faced with situations that cause fear, worry, and anxiety. At each stage of development, whether in toddlerhood or middle age, we need to face problems and threats (actual and potential) to our being, our livelihood, our relationships, our wellness.

Infants are in danger of mistrust. Toddlers can be burdened by shame and guilt. School age children can be made to feel inferior. Teens can become confused about who and what they want to be. Young adults can fall into isolation and loneliness. Mid-life can cause us to become stagnant. Old age can bring on despair. Without an organizing principle that aligns with these potential downfalls, we and our family members' successful maturation can be compromised. If we get stuck and do not move through each stage, we will experience disintegration emotionally, relationally, spiritually, mentally, and even physically.

Being Alive

A growth-centered family is alive. It grows, and this growth is rooted with capabilities to learn and lead effectively through the challenging complexities of evolution and expansion. Growth is the business of a family. It's the reason behind all the good we want for our kids. Yes, love, happiness, care, responsibility, and protection are all important essentials, but they can actually become stumbling blocks when they're not empowering individuals to grow how they love, create, care, respond, lead, learn, and protect.

What will achieve more of the most meaningful outcomes of deeper, heartfelt bonds, developing world-changing character, and legacy-level success? Life. Not just making a living or having a life, but being alive!

What qualifies something as alive? Movement. "Living organisms are distinguished from nonliving entities by the fact that they move; they are animated."[6] On an everyday level, this means we are moving through stages of development—physically, emotionally, vocationally, relationally, professionally, spiritually. In other words, growth. If we're not moving in this manner, we're likely stagnant and just going through the motions. Can anyone say zombie?

Recall Erikson's stages of psychosocial development (Chapter 3). Each level involved a primary challenge or crisis to overcome in order to achieve certain virtues. If successful, one can move upward and forward to the next—that is, become more mature. In the early years, success is almost entirely dependent on the child's environment. A foundation of trust supports the development of autonomy and initiative through the toddler years to four or five. The challenge is actually in the hands of the parents. Will they cultivate a home with stability, affection, and safety? Once our kids start going to school, they will be spending significantly more and more time away from us. If they have been fortified with trust, the ability to function independently, and openness to new experiences, they will be much more prepared to navigate the rigors of learning and application. Then comes the seven- to ten-year

---

[6] *Biology of Belief*, Bruce Lipton, 2007, p.32.

process of becoming an adult, growing their own identity as they become more and more aware of their personality, capacities, inclinations, strengths, and weaknesses.

This is where things get hairy and complicated. Puberty and adolescence is a profound metamorphosis involving many diverse parts of us. But one area that may often be overlooked is that of meaning making—i.e., how we interpret our sensory data and ongoing story to produce an ideology that will be running things in the background, like an operating system. This is actually the primary thrust of this book—to be a parent who can effectively facilitate and even liberate those they lovingly oversee to develop healthy, empowered ways of being and doing. To be growth-centered, so that over the course of eighteen or so years, children move toward adulthood while discovering self, purpose, integration, and fulfillment. This movement is an important indicator that one is truly alive—that mind, heart, and soul are becoming more developed and integrated as a whole.

What moves us positively through the stages? Love. But it's not your garden variety love, which is often constrained by outdated, limiting rules and beliefs. The rest of this section goes on to define this dynamic, bonding force that liberates us to consistently move toward a life of wholeness.

Considering Erikson's bookends of trusting and being trustworthy, our lives are meant to be filled with movement. We move from a place of trust to being autonomous to exercising initiative and industriousness. We discover who and what we really are in order to grow intimacy with another person, thereby generating new life and positive change. We integrate our purposes and experiences into a profound, unified story. On this road to maturation, it is essential to move from a secure foundation of physical health and safety, with supportive relationships and healthy esteem, to being a lifelong learner, aligned in mind and heart, empowered with deep knowledge, leading with wisdom and vision. In this way, we bring about higher levels of being and doing for future generations.[7]

This powerful shift involves deep personal transformation. The teen years and early twenties are when this happens, unless derailed by fear-based choices caused by societal pressures to conform and dysfunctional relationships with parents. Becoming mature is not just getting bigger, more knowledgeable, and more responsible; it is a deconstruction and reorganization of being and doing as a child, especially meaning making.

Here's my own journey. I was an only child, immigrating to the United States in 1971. My parents struggled to make a new life for us, and I had numerous setbacks in my development. First was my mother leaving me and my dad when I was three to come to America. I was without her for two years. My therapist friends tell me that was a big hit to my autonomy and initiative. The second setback was skipping second grade when I transferred from a public school to private. My mom actually doesn't remember why, but it happened. In third grade, my grades nosedived, and so did my self-esteem since my classmates were

---

[7] https://www.valuescentre.com/mapping-values/barrett-model/stages-psychological-development

bigger, faster, smarter, and more mature. A third occurred in fifth grade, when my dad decided to move us to Australia for sentimental reasons, only to move us back six months later because things didn't pan out and my mother couldn't stand it. I was uprooted twice in less than a year.

I think all this eventually erupted as rebellion in my late teens and early twenties. I burned close relationships (including with my parents), crashed a motorcycle, and flipped a car. In the midst of all this, I didn't have conversations to process thoughts and feelings. Looking back, my lack of success makes sense. I had developmental needs that weren't being met, and I simply managed it the best I knew how—by not being motivated or ambitious. I didn't have the knowledge and confidence in myself to pursue any conventional goals. I think this had to do with competition, not believing I could win when so many others were much more able.

But reflecting on all this, what seemed disadvantageous led me to reject what everybody else was doing and turn to God for a different foundation, a different center. At the age of twenty, I committed to finding out what the God of the Bible wanted for me, rather than what others were telling me, including family, friends, even the pastors and leaders at my church.

This spiritual quest involved working at the church's summer day camp, serving in numerous ministries, regularly attending worship services, and being a part of a fellowship. As beneficial as those were, the primary core of my growth came from reading the Bible from cover to cover many times and applying it to effect my intrapersonal and interpersonal character: taking what I read and interacting with existing beliefs, values, attitudes and behaviors. And when I accepted and embraced what I read but found my own ways of thinking and doing contrary, I made decisions to reject and replace my ideology with a growing worldview that I found much more organized around love and relationships. This definitely didn't happen overnight though there were times of awakening; but mostly, it was a process of acceptance of a belief and having it tested in the crucible of relationships, at work and home. And with the panoply of Biblical content, my thinking, my life my philosophy, and my ideology was shaped around the revelations of the God who became a human being and embodied a countercultural organizing principle. The synthesis of the foreshadowing, descriptions, and expressions of Jesus Christ in the Old Testament and the narratives and epistles of the New Testament formed a way for me to understand God, myself, and life that was different than anything I had heard anywhere else—from parents, friends, and yes, even church.

God was profoundly defined by love, and I wanted Him to be my foundation and source of change. When I considered my way of being, thinking, and doing after two decades of life, I saw very clearly that this love was foreign to me. As I sought to love in this new way, my relationship with God grew dynamically because it was so challenging yet freeing. The source of my transformation was God, and the conduit was the new beliefs, values, and rules I developed as I practiced thinking and doing according to profoundly defined love.

This journey has a continual, daily effect on the meaning I make from the things I see, hear, and feel. It has been cathartic, redemptive, and edifying. It has centered my life on growth and the fostering of what matters most—connection, not only to what's positive, but also to the hard, painful things. I don't avoid difficult, frightening challenges, but rather stay open to learning and becoming more mature in how I view and engage adversity.

Transforming to become uniquely who we are and what we were made for comes from letting go of those perceptions given to us as young people, before we could evaluate their merits and decide if they were really something we wanted. As long as our perceptions, default beliefs, values, and rules are primarily controlling the way we manage our lives, we will not become mature.

Liberation at this level is the path less taken. It is arduous. It takes time. And if it involves dealing with our parents' failed strategies, we need healing as well. Ultimately, to become the person we were made to be, we need to break free from outdated, inferior, unnecessarily limiting beliefs about who we are and what life's about. And to not leave this up for grabs, it is about being a parent whose purpose is to create and cultivate a home that empowers everyone to make wise decisions for long-term thriving.

Nature has plenty of transformative examples of life movement. Look at a tree: it starts off as a nut, which doesn't look like much (zero resemblance to a tree). But it contains everything it needs to interact with its environment to become a healthy organism. If it lands in a life-conducive environment, it will become animated and grow to establish preconditions for the eventual growth and functions of its mature state.

A nut's goal of becoming a tree is its miraculous vision. To move toward that outcome, there is tremendous movement below the ground as roots reach out in all directions, anchoring the tree and receiving what it needs. As it germinates, stems, branches, and leaves emerge and reach toward the light it needs to continue becoming what it was created to be. In its mature state, it will implement an incredible scaled-up process: giving us oxygen, possibly delicious fruit, shelter to animals and foliage, even multiplying itself many times over.

What makes the future possible is the nut's underground growth— its network of roots contribute to maximizing surface area for respiration, excretion, and intake of nutrients. Every part works together to promote growth and prepare for maturation. But none of this is visible to the world; the creation of this life-giving foundation goes on underground. Although it's unseen, the preconditions are absolutely essential and critical for the scaling up that will occur above the surface. If we want a healthy, long-lived tree, we don't want to confine or contaminate the soil. A vibrant, healthy root system is what keeps it alive season after season, keeping it firmly planted in a life-sustaining relationship with the earth.

One more observation about the life movement of a tree—there is an incredible transformation from a nut to an incredibly complex organism of trunk, branches, leaves, and fruit. The significance of transformation is obvious, yet is often overlooked in the healthy growth of living things. A nut looks nothing like a tree, or any part of the tree other than another nut. And it doesn't function like any other part, either. In other words, there's not a linear, observable progression where we can see similarities between seed and sapling. Radical change starts with blueprints, and it's the presence of life-giving elements that enables the internal instructions to be implemented.

Likewise, our families need cultivation of healthy conditions to develop the connections, capacities, strengths, and skills for every member to scale up. Healthy, successful organisms (cells, trees, etc.) are prime examples for organizations (families, corporations, nonprofits) to follow. Just like the interaction between roots and soil in our tree example, the environment and connections cultivated by parents' decisions establish the preconditions for scaling up. Without them, sustainable growth will not occur. This is an essential alignment to life, and it is achieved when we center on growth and function in ways that are conducive to its promotion. This centering occurs mostly out of sight. The most significant, radical growths of each of our family members is hidden from our view, as well. But if we create healthy, empowering preconditions, we'll be blessed with experiencing the manifestations and expressions of growth. And in time, we'll see our spouse and children in their mature states, implementing an incredible scaling up process—inspiring those they touch, bringing them joy, creating safe places around them, and eventually multiplying goodness many times over for their families and communities.

If we're going to create healthy cultures, we, too, need to align with life. We need to continue on our path to maturation. We need energy, skills, and tools to establish preconditions for scaling up. This means treating emotional injuries with gritty work on our beliefs and perspectives. It also means creating structure in our lives for regular rest and recreation to balance work and stress. Even more importantly, it's prioritizing our relationships and their health so that we're not overdoing things *for* our loved ones, but rather *with* them. I go deeper into these subjects in Part Three. This collective work will create the network of underground (unseen by the world) connections to support aboveground development and maturation that the world will see and be blessed by. I believe it is the internal health and vitality that enlightens, inspires, and energizes people to authentic greatness, and in turn, brings long-term benefits to all those they love and serve.

A growth-centered family grows and progresses positively through the stages of life. It's not always smooth, but a s surely as mistakes and challenges are encountered, learning happens, changes and course corrections are made. Parents function and behave in ways that effectively meet the needs of each other and the children so they can grow, too. This occurs mostly out of sight to the world. But when our homes are healthy with empowering preconditions, we'll be blessed with the manifestations and expressions of each person's maturation.

Chapter 7: Empowering Relationships

A growth-centered family is a network of dynamic relationships that empowers each member to continually develop, adapt, and contribute in ever-increasingly significant ways. This kind of network is the precondition we want to establish—that which prepares its members to scale up effectively into their highest, most meaningful potentials.

We have eighteen years of scaling up with our children. As parents, we might focus on education, physical provisions, and finances. Yet, as important as those are, if we want our family members to thrive, those responsibilities don't help us tackle complex growth. The #1 thing that must be central and consistently prioritized is the health of our relationships. They need to foster development of healthy leadership (for both parents and kids), providing high levels of challenge and support . These kinds of connections are what empower us to become what we are meant to. How we connect, encourage, challenge, communicate, care, and resolve conflict determines how we will effectively lead our families through the difficulties and dangers of complex growth. If each line of communication improves in this way, our family will be ready for the stormy seas of scaling up.

I'm sure you have goals for your family. How's your plan looking? And how about its execution? To be successful, you need to align with the dynamic constants of time and life. Alignment means substantial prioritization for growth—equal or more attention and time than we give to responsibilities of productivity. How much are you investing into your relationships and the leadership development for your family's success?

Viewing psychosocial stages with the concept of preconditions helps us see the significance of relationships. When our families are centered on growth, the environment of healthy relationships is prioritized above all else. This enables, and even empowers each member to successfully navigate the stage they're in. Is your family a place where every member is growing the wisdom to deal with the complexities of the stages they're in?

For little people, under age seven, their growing wisdom is mostly about downloading information from their environment. This will form the foundation of trust, autonomy, and initiative. If parents provide the stability of deep affection and emotionally healthy love, precious ones will feel safe and have open channels for learning. Learning motivates them to explore and find out more about their world. If the world is interesting, safe, and loving, they gain the courage and confidence to initiate rather than wait for others to go first. Together with training in boundaries, children develop the perception to discern opportunities and limits, and move forward successfully. This is especially important in relationships, because loving well requires this dynamic dance of giving and receiving, communicating honestly and respectfully from the heart. This is foundational.

For K-12th grade students, wisdom involves development of industry and identity. Industry strengthens cognitive abilities and skills for greater discernment, processing, and expression. Of course, this is intended to prepare one for the workforce, but stronger thinking is needed to navigate relational and emotional complexities. This is a new area of content for many of our pre-college educational systems, but fortunately, it is being developed and implemented by healthy, forward-thinking educational leaders. If heart and head are growing, youth will be more ready for the decade-long challenge of discovering and determining who they are and what they want to be as adults. This is especially significant for long-term commitment relationships.

When I married at twenty-five, I didn't know much about anything, literally. I proposed over the phone. Didn't help my wife plan the wedding. The first year or two, I failed to spend time working on our relationship or taking care of home maintenance. I did want to be the best husband, but I was incredibly ignorant and immature. I'm so glad my wife helped me realize things that I needed to change. I did initially resist, coming up with excuses and justifications, but did enough introspection to challenge my priorities, and realign them to prove my love was true. This wasn't easy. Pride was swallowed, but it I was clearer about what I was and what I needed to do to become who I wanted to be.

When we have matured emotionally with healthy boundaries and trust, we are more aware of what is beneficial in the long run. Without robust development in head and heart, we are left with uncontrollable vortexes that drive our lives into mismanagement and chaos.

As we move into young adulthood, we need to be able to grow intimacy in our closest relationships that will continue to evolve us into a generative person in our middle adult years. These two virtues of maturation contribute to our success and fulfillment. We're able to build appropriate, healthy trust, and thus able to make a real difference in those we live and work with. These abilities are key factors in effective, satisfying collaboration that brings effective, innovative improvements and benefits to others.

If I hadn't grown through the challenges of the first few years of my marriage, I don't think I would've developed the character needed to cultivate greater intimacy with my beloved wife. As we struggled to start a family, eventually bringing in our beautiful first born, we were able to be there for each other physically and emotionally, connecting through the tears and joys our amazing daughter brought. The environment of our home was filled with emotional and physical closeness that greatly helped us bond as a family. Our second child came two years later and our joyful intimacy continued.

Meanwhile, as I worked with middle school and high school students, my organizing principle was evolving to center me on virtues that helped me authentically and effectively connect with my students. When I first started as a teacher, I was too nice. Then I swung the other way and became too strict. After the third or fourth year, I was finding a middle ground. I learned to be more patient and kind, but more importantly, what I discovered throughout this learning curve, is that I was getting to know what was truly going on with each person and situation, whether it had to do with pedagogy or discipline, and this is what has made the difference. This meant asking more and better questions to gain insight into where my students were. But equally important was knowing myself; without substantial self-awareness, my perceptions and decisions would not be equitable. Jesus puts it this way,

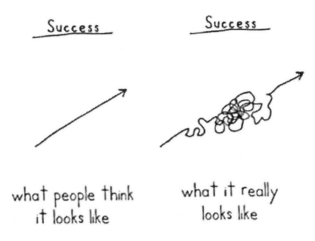

Success   Success

what people think   what it really
it looks like   looks like

"You hypocrite, first take the plank out of your own eye, and then you will see clearly to remove the speck from your brother's eye" (Matthew 7:5). This kind of intimacy set the stage for me to discover what would help me be generative, not only at work but also at home.

Then comes the mature stage of integrity, consisting of the ability to make cohesive sense of all things good and bad, joy and pain, achievements and losses. Achieving this virtue gives us the consistency of character and depth of wisdom to lead our families and organizations to positively transform the world. If we want every family member to mature, we need all our relationships to be as healthy as possible—especially the relationship we see between our parents, as they cultivate the environment of relationships.

Relationships and Success

Success is not linear, but rather full of twists, turns, and switchbacks. All these curves represent choices, trials, mistakes, failures, new choices, more attempts, disappointments, and so on. What determines the direction is what we learn, how we change, how we prioritize differently, and how we continue to grow. We want success for ourselves and our children, but oftentimes we're not consciously aware of the actual path—the one with all the twists that cause us to feel off-course. Going off course is integral to finding success, but do we have the relationships to help us figure out the why's, how's, and what's next?. *That* is where the growth happens.

Richard St. John, through interviews with highly successful people as well as his own successes, has identified these eight traits: passion, work, focus, push, ideas, improvement, service, and persistence. All eight are needed, but to generate and foster them, we need to cultivate the preconditions by prioritizing growth of healthy relationships.

Healthy relationships give life to our hearts, the source of those eight traits. Our heart is about how we perceive and feel about others and ourselves and circulating those contents to our entire being. A thriving heart fuels passion, purpose, and hope, shaping us to become all we can be. Heart-life is the animation of our greatest desires, our top and most fulfilling goal. It's being moved by passion and inspiration to use our greatest strengths to change the world with attitudes and actions reflecting the true worth of human beings. It's what our kids need most.

Healthy heart connections move them from stage to stage toward maturity. Relationships that give heart-life create the preconditions for meaningful work with ongoing focus, push, ideas, improvement, service, and persistence.

We need to be aware of how our parenting shapes our relationships with our kids, and how the relationships influence the development of their minds and hearts. Common parenting styles which are not helpful are when we act as helicopters or drill sergeants. When we relate to our kids as helicopters, hovering and rescuing, we debilitate their resourcefulness and ability to solve problems. Overprotection robs them of the satisfaction of finding internal sufficiency and the capability to overcome difficulties, create opportunities, or take advantage of them. Whether they're experiencing consequences of poor choices, not listening and following instructions, or forgetting to take care of a responsibility, our children do not need micromanagement.

Of course, I need to point out here the difference between affordable mistakes versus ones that can cause long-term disabilities and irreparable harm. Too often, parents don't make intelligent, rational distinctions—they think everything that causes emotional distress unaffordable. This symptom could be an indicator of a parent's unmet needs for security, love and belonging, and maybe even esteem. Or perhaps it's even more basic; they just need to improve the meeting of their physiological needs, i.e. sleep, diet, excretion, etc.

If we don't stop helicoptering, our kids may be at risk of lacking responsibility, decreased ability to learn from life, and poor decision-making skills.

When we show up as drill sergeants, we diminish our children's ability to hear their own voice and discover their own creativity, beauty, and strength. Whether as helicopters and drill sergeants, we have good intentions, and we may be helpful at times. But more often than not, we're not doing anything that liberates our children to develop into loving, strong, resilient, courageous, lifelong learners.

Relationships create the environment which either fosters openness to learning and application or rejection of help and support. Not many of us are born with all eight elements. Mostly, they are acquired over time, which means it is absolutely critical that we are open to adopting and applying them. This openness of mind and heart is generated by authentic trust-building, secure, cherishing love. Its opposite is fear that fosters worry, anxiety, greed, and sacrifice of relationships.

Relationships, Not Money

Conventionally, money and fame have been thought to be great contributors to happiness. The Harvard Study of Adult Life begs to differ. In a seventy-year study of 724 men, the data revealed that good relationships are the most important thing in determining health and happiness, not money.

Here are some great findings:

1. Social connections are really good for us; loneliness kills and is actually toxic.

2. High quality close relationships—without toxic, high conflict but rather consistent, warm affection—protect our health. The happiest and most satisfied people in close relationships in their fifties were healthiest and happiest at eighty.

3. Good relationships protect our brains; those with secure attachments at eighty had the highest brain function.

This is not new, but why is it not more consistently prioritized, and more universally communicated? Probably because relationship work is messy and complicated; it's not a quick fix or sexy. It's more difficult to quantify, and doesn't initially appear as profitable.

What happens when you replace screen time with people time? It was amazing what happened in my family when we banned the kids' phones for a day and came up with positive and constructive activities. This was possible because of healthy relationships. Our brains were open to thinking of things we could do rather than allow our fight/flight responses hijack the day. Start taking walks together, once a week and build from there. Consistently prioritizing a personal activity creates great potential for a healthier relationship.

It's no surprise that high relational health also transfers over to work. Jeremie Kubicek of Giant Worldwide Consulting recently said this: "Relational intelligence is the future competitive advantage for leaders.

In the new world the capacity to establish, develop, and maintain key relationships both inside and outside your organization is going to become the primary currency of leadership influence."

Productivity must no longer be the sole focus of great leadership. Bosses being disconnected from those they lead is unacceptable. Aren't you tired of moms and dads not being present with their children? What about the lack of awareness that comes from busy adults married to tasks and missing out on the real moments that define life?

The time to elevate the value of strong, healthy relationships is way overdue. Are you investing enough to effectively and substantially grow this most important area of life for your health, your happiness, your longevity, your family, your organization/company?

A growth-centered family cultivates an environment of relationships which grow a healthy foundation. This is most important the first six to seven years of a child's life, when they are in the downloading phase of their development. This foundational time can empower their souls for the next stages, or it can diminish their capacities and abilities.

Teaching Healthy Relationships

In Alpha International's Parenting Children Course[8], there's a great section on teaching relationships. This is a primary role for parents. This of course begins with listening, a foundational element of healthy relationships. When we're with our loved ones, we need to pay full attention to recognize the importance of the moment. This means ceasing to think about whatever else you've got going and shifting your focus. Much of your ability to do this depends on your interior life management.

Maintaining eye contact helps your listening—not constant, because that'd be weird, but with consistency throughout your time together. In addition, show interest by putting forth effort and giving generous amounts of time to get to know what your precious ones are interested in. Make sure you don't censor their sharing with value judgments. Avoid shutting them down by devaluing their ideas and interests. Allow them to express negative feelings like disappointment, embarrassment, sadness, anxiety, and anger. A healthy interior will also help you to be more accepting and open to your loved ones being different from you.

As you listen, reflect back what you hear. Repeat back to your child what you think he or she is saying. Paraphrase—use some of their words; don't be a parrot. Show you're trying to understand accurately with genuine interest and lack of criticism. Then, when appropriate,

---

[8] The Parenting Children's Course (Alpha International, 2011), pp.47-52.

take things to another level by reflecting back the feelings you think your child is trying to express, like "It sounds like you feel upset/frustrated/sad?" This requires even more empty-mindedness from you, but demonstrates your presence. In addition to authentically listening and getting to know the one you love, you're also helping them identify their own feelings and grow awareness of their interior. This is a great boost to their ongoing development.

Foster Healthy Relational Space

In addition to listening and being present, we want to facilitate health in the relationships our kids have with other members of the family. This involves doing some things and not doing others. We don't want to compare. We don't want to get involved in every conflict. But we do want to have regular time as a family. We want to give each child their own space and privacy. And we definitely want to help our kids develop health in their interior lives.

1. *Don't compare.* Value each child's uniqueness and avoid labeling. Don't contrast to make one look better to motivate the other to improve. Work individually for their own development and not some archaic, traditional, or generic valuation. Help each child improve in how they get their needs met, managing their time, progress, and results. When they are equipped and encouraged to evaluate

themselves and decide how they want to grow, they will be empowered to discover and act upon opportunities with their God-given strengths.

2. *Don't try to arbitrate every fight your kids get into.* Give them space to work out their own disagreements. Remain impartial—don't automatically blame the older child or expect them to be more responsible, and don't jump to conclusions without due diligence. Intervene if they're hurting each other or one is dominating the dialogue. We don't want to allow bullying, unkind words, or vicious attacks. Be a mentor and coach. Help them think about what will help them get better at tense conversations. Equip them with skills and tools to grow their ability and capacity as peacemakers.

3. *Have time together as a family.* Relationships need this, and plenty of it—usually more than we think. Don't drift into eating separately, especially as the kids get older. Don't have several TVs in the house, and don't allow members to always be on separate screens. Put effort into everyone getting good at managing their screen time. This will likely be messy, but recall from the boundaries section that how we deal with this can be a great culture boost.

4. *Organize family nights, outings, vacations.* Get them on the calendar. Do chores together. Be spontaneous in having fun together, playing childish games, being silly, playing outside. Don't always entertain them or provide something for them to do; allow them to be bored so they make up their own games activities. Patiently persevere in finding ways to have fun together and enjoy each other.

5. *Give each child space and some privacy.* Recognize that some children need more alone time than others, and that this need changes as they get older. They need me time to learn how to slow down, reflect, be introspective, develop their own identity (story, values, boundaries, vision) without externals (people, activities, environments) unnecessarily getting their attention and possibly directing them in ways that do not draw the best out of them. Of course, some externals are incredibly beneficial. But without down time, being overly busy and tired decreases their capacity to discern what to let in and what to do without. Meeting this need also helps them with the next point.

6. *Help them develop empathy and see each other's good points.* Foster the responsibility to look out for each other, appreciate each other, recognize each other's strengths and differences. Encourage them to think about how the other feels and to put themselves in that space. Ultimately, this grows relationships that sincerely honor and support each other. This brings us back to the need to prioritize the soul and development of the interior life, growing awareness and energy that supports perennial movement in the fulfilling maturation process. Developing empathy and strong, loving character requires consistent attention, intention, and repetition of what matters most—cultivating a growth centered family.

Equally important are emotions. We need to understand them as powerful and immediate affecters of behavior. To grow our parenting skills, we need to respond to our children's negative behavior with an understanding of how their emotions drive their actions. If we neglect this area, we indirectly teach our kids to ignore this potent force. We create habits of unawareness that profoundly impact how they lead and manage their lives as adults. We also need to know how to foster strong, positive emotional bonds with our kids and make it a regular part of our home culture. We want them to feel good when they think of their family and home environment.

This brings us to the radical, vital element to being growth centered —perception. Our emotions flow from our perceptions—how we view situations, others, and especially ourselves. Over time, our perceptions develop the stories we tell ourselves. These stories reflect the meaning we make from the things we see and hear on a daily basis. They grow in power as they get stored in our subconscious and become the source of how we lead and manage our lives. The amazing power of the subconscious, able to process a million times more bits of data than our conscious mind, takes all our experiences, perceptions, and stories to create a comprehensive, subjective worldview. This is what enables us to do much of what we do without much effort and thought. It's efficient, but it can be a double-edged sword, fast tracking us toward success or devastation.

The Place & Power of Perception

Perception is at the root of life. How we see and interpret the things happening around us and to us can produce happiness or hostility, love or loneliness, contentment or contention. If we believe the world is a safe place and the people in our lives care deeply about us, if we value ourselves and what we possess—both the tangible and intangible—we will have hope. We will develop the gratitude and grace to make wise decisions that benefit others and ourselves. The more pervasive these beliefs are, the more we learn about the myriad of problems and complexities that come with being human. We are open to the challenges and opportunities that come our way to positively contribute to the wellness and growth of society.

Stop and think about how perceptions drive behavior. If there's danger, the fight or flight response generally gets triggered. If things are well, there's tendency to relax and let the guard down. This is fine as long as conditions are accurately perceived. It's when there's misinterpretation that things become chaotic, and possibly even destructive. When there's no danger and yet we prepare for war, we will likely cause harm and damage. Conversely, if harm is imminent and we are unaware, we experience significant loss.

But there's something that controls our perception-making—our souls. The condition of our souls directly affects how we see and explicate. If healthy, we will have the courage and compassion to examine and evaluate honestly. We won't avoid the messiness and pain of relationship problems. We will make the effort to become people who care enough to be candid and respectful. We will have the patience and kindness to be truly helpful to those struggling, whether it's a family member or someone we serve vocationally. It can even be ourselves; at some point, we all get overwhelmed, needing recovery and restoration.

If our souls are not well, we are controlled by fear and a sense that there's never enough—not enough time, money, or resources. Not enough goodness in the world. This can easily drive thoughts and feelings of being not smart enough, not good enough, not doing enough, not having enough. When you boil this down, it's simply that we're not enough. Our beliefs perpetuate profound perceptions of scarcity. When all this is embedded in our subconscious, this infused sense of deficiency and inferiority is both potent and difficult to detect. We need to grow our awareness of what our soul is and how to help it thrive.

Much of the tactical information I share in the third part of this book is intended to grow motivation and skills, strengthening and developing the inner life to connect with that of others. Healthy relationships require decisions, actions, and commitments that prioritize the emotional and spiritual wellness of mind and heart. Perceptions drive decision, actions, commitments, and prioritization. And it's the soul that determines how we comprehend life and the world to do what's needed to truly empower our relationships.

Wanted: Men with Emotional Muscles

But there's one more thing about relationships before I wrap up this chapter—men and relationships. Do you know just how important a man's actions are? The success of marriage and family relationships critically depends on the male, i.e. the husband and father. We need more men who passionately care about higher levels of emotional health and deeper levels of understanding the hidden challenges and solutions of loving well.

In *Time*'s 2016 June issue, Belinda Luscombe reported in addition to other findings, "...men need to do more of the 'emotional labor' in a relationship—work going into sustaining love; 'What men do in a relationship is, by a large margin, the crucial factor that separates a great relationship from a failed one,' contributed John Gottman (national leading marriage expert). A man's actions are the key variable that determines whether a relationship succeeds or fails."

This is a primary area of leadership for men. In the past, preoccupation with male leadership has had many negative repercussions, especially for work cultures, not to speak of the effects at home. I've seen it over and over again—when men take up the helm in fostering healthy relationships and emotional maturity, everything and everyone benefits, especially the man himself. Conversely, when the complexities of inner life change and growth are not prioritized and embraced, potentials are not realized, purpose is not fulfilled, direction is not clear, and passion is lost. This is true not only in marriage and family, but organizations as well.

Thank God more and more leaders are seeing, understanding and pursuing this positive evolution. Regardless of your gender, becoming more aware, attentive, and action-oriented toward heart work revolutionizes your life and results in greater health and fortitude in all dimensions—personal, professional, physical, emotional, spiritual, and on and on. Whether you're single, married, divorced, retired, or any other life stage, or you're CEO, ED, manager, employee, or any other role in an organization, don't live without clarity and commitment to the essential foundation of a growth-centered ideology and practice. It is the keystone of a thriving life.

Family life is incredibly dynamic, and it takes a lot of wisdom and strength to successfully navigate marriage, parenting, and life after kids —to ultimately leave a profound, transformative legacy. Being growth-centered doesn't leave this highest priority up to chance. Elevating the value of lifelong learning simply makes sense, and it will go a long way in preparing for all the storms ahead. And there is great reward and joy in making it through in one piece, intact, "till death do us part." The reward is in the arduous journey transforming our contexts to make sense of our history. It is experiencing the fulfillment of understanding and achieving a beautiful life, unique and precious in unity with the One who created it and gave it to us.

Being growth-centered is absolutely essential to fulfill our vows of love to our spouses, our children, their children, and beyond. And men have a profound, critical, and even transcendent role in this. A growth-centered man is a radical source of a world being freed from scarcity to sufficiency.

Let's put some flesh on this by thinking about parenting teens. How do you want to parent your children when they become teens? Want to be close or distant? Strict or lenient? Controlling or freeing? Trusting or suspicious? I think the best thing is not being "or" anything. As much as possible, be an "and" parent. Strict and lenient. Trusting and suspicious. Loving and powerful. Gentle and firm. Fun and serious. Hands off and on. And just because we have both, it doesn't mean equal amounts of both. The amounts never remain static; we draw upon different quantities depending on the situation. But how do we determine how much and when?

This is about having relationships that balance challenge *and* support. It's showing up honestly and respectfully, securely connecting to others and being appropriately independent. It's being present and productive. It doesn't matter whether it's with your child, your boss, your employee, your business partner, your spouse, or your best friend. For these relationships to thrive, we've got to do "and" well. But how? To this we turn in the next chapter.

Chapter 8: Soulful

Aligning with time and life helps us value and prioritize our relationships. In order to translate that into real, regular action, we need to care for our souls. A growth-centered family cares deeply about the soul of each member. The soul is the deepest, most important part of us because it integrates us internally to deeply, meaningfully connect with our loved ones. When our souls are well, we can challenge and support each other to generate and foster liberating relationships. When our kids lack challenge, they miss out on strong development physically, emotionally, mentally, and spiritually; without support, they can get discouraged, apathetic, and desperate. So, what exactly is the soul, and how do we care for it?

Our souls are critically important; they are the connectors, our CAOs (Chief And Officer). Healthy souls create healthy relationships, which create healthy cultures. Functioning like the operating system of a computer, it connects everything about us so we can live, love, and work seamlessly, effectively, and powerfully. Our souls are intended to help us prioritize, process, integrate, determine, and execute tasks, actions, and behaviors to achieve success and fulfillment in the things that matter most to us. When our souls are well, our lives move forward as we experience ups and downs, encounter challenges, and find resolutions. When our souls aren't healthy, we get stuck—or worse, regress in our positive development as humans. Our relationships suffer, and we miss out on opportunities for greater impact, joy, contributions, and meaning.

In addition to being an operating system, your soul is your interpreter of data and the writer of your life's story. This story is not simply *about* you; it *is* you (John Holmes, PhD, psychology professor, Waterloo University)[9]. A thriving soul takes in millions of bits of data, positive and negative, joyful and painful, to create a story full of drama, adventure, courage, sacrifice, and redemption. The intensity and power of triumphs and traumas come together to produce a profound story, unique, dynamic, and glorious. Moreover, lifelong, authentic, loving relationships and communities are the result of these kinds of stories coming together, creating even greater stories of deep, meaningful connection.

A blessed soul makes sense of all things and fits them into an ever-evolving paradigm. And in each stage, our desires, struggles, crises, resolutions, and behaviors reveal a new person empowered to engage problems, find solutions, and contribute positively to those around them. This begins with intrapersonal challenges, to those in their family, and then continues on into their workplace, communities, and even the world.

The soul is what empowers us to lead our will, mind, and body. When our soul is not well, we fall into bad habits and patterns and our wills and minds don't stand a chance against. Our body's unmet needs will manifest as addictions, enslaving us to disintegrating ways of thinking and doing.

What does a soul need to thrive? Fundamentally, the nature of the soul is to need. In *Soul Keeping*, John Ortberg explains that there are

---

[9] American Psychological Association, http://www.apa.org/monitor/2011/01/stories.aspx

numerous things our souls need. His list of needs is rest, a father, satisfaction, hope, a future, a center, freedom, a keeper, blessing, gratitude, and to be with God. If we try to not need, we neglect our souls. Are you getting your soul needs met? Write those needs down and score them 1 to 5 (1 being not met, 5 being fully met) to get a picture of how your soul might be doing. Then, come up with things you want to do to better care for your soul. Here are some suggestions to raise your scores:

- "Ruthlessly eliminate hurry."—Dallas Willard (American philosopher known for his writings on Christian spiritual formation). On one level, this is a matter of managing your calendar. But more profoundly, it's a choice. It is honoring healthy limits. It's replacing default beliefs and rules about success, love, and fulfillment to prioritize what matters most in the long term.

- When you create space and time, you become open to the possibilities of a healthier soul. So, make a list of soul-restoring activities, beginning with rest and followed by social connections, personal stimulations, virtuous pursuits, and solitude retreats. There's no rush to implement, but commit to their execution in the next ninety days. Put them in your calendar.

- As your soul gets stronger, you experience greater integration of being and doing, heart and mind. With continued elimination of hurry, clarify and develop your long-term, top-level, highest goal—what you're truly about. It could be your spirituality, the kind of parent you want to be, the marriage you want to have, the fitness and overall health you want to develop, the legacy you want to leave.

This commitment will involve making time to do different things. It means subtracting before adding. What's causing fatigue, chronic stress, and exhaustion? Determine not only the activities, but also the instinctual beliefs and rules that are driving your choices. These need to be replaced with ones that generate win-wins. That means choices that help you find greater support and resources, i.e. solutions that come from courageous and compassionate perceptions. This comes from and contributes to higher levels of psychological wisdom and emotional health. Ultimately, it results in a growth center that supports our family members and us to become mature in how we love and do life.

Soul Need: A Center

Out of all the needs that Ortberg described, I want to focus on our need for a center, a growth center—a *massive center* that is able to sustain a life-generating culture of healthy relationships for a lifetime and beyond. At the beginning of this book, I started with centers; they organize us and set priorities. But without a centered soul, our unifying principle will be lacking and the milieu of our family compromised by stress and busyness, resulting in unhealthy relationships and immature emotional development. Most, if not all families want fulfillment and success for their children. In order to achieve these outcomes, parents elevate certain priorities, the obvious being a place to live, income for expenses, and education for the kids. But as I said in chapter one, these cannot be central. They meet certain needs, but if they are deemed the things that matter most, we miss out on the intangibles that enlighten, encourage, and empower us to become healthy lovers, wise parents, great decision makers, problem solvers, innovative creators, gritty, passionate, persevere people. True love doesn't just happen and endure because we have our physical needs met. Relationships don't flourish just because we have a high-paying job and a beautiful house. A family centered on growth and generating a healthy culture is powered by individuals whose soul is centered on something much more than the tangible.

The solar system is a great example of something generating this kind of culture, where something way bigger is at the center and much smaller things revolve around it. This system has sustained life for as long as we've known it; many generations have come and gone, and our solar system has provided conditions for life—even human life—to continue. It's allowed people to evolve in numerous aspects to develop and learn from failures and successes. When we learn to cultivate love, societies and nations move forward into higher levels of mastery, stewardship, and compassion. When we hold onto fear, we become monsters, destroying others and ourselves.

If we want to be part of a forward fulfillment universe, we need this kind of center in our own "solar system." What does it take to sustain a life-generating system?

A sun. Our primary source of light and warmth. It enables us to see and perpetually energizes every atom of our world. Without it, we would be blind and frozen. Planets would drift off into space. We and our precious Earth would perish if it weren't for the sun's gravity and energy.

How massive does a center need to be to keep things intact? To keep us in orbit (along with the others), the sun has 109 times the diameter of earth and has a mass about 333,000 times as much. Approximately 1,300,000 Earths can fit in the sun!

For life as we know it to exist, this ginormous, gaseous center gives us visibility and warmth. We're able to see what's going on and make sense of it so we can figure out what we need and want to do to survive and thrive (aka, observing, theorizing, planning, experimenting, problem solving, etc.). Seeing is absolutely essential. And having light consistently day after day, year after year, generation to generation has promoted our existence and evolution as a species. Let's not forget about the life-conducive temperatures we experience; yes, we get cold and hot, but not beyond the limits we can endure or protect ourselves from.

Do we have something like this at the center of our system?

Just as the sun is the source of life, there's something that energizes our souls to foster a growth-centered family. What exactly would this center be for us?

It's love—a love represented by the sun and its system of planets. Our solar system is a model for us to follow. Our most painful and challenging problems defeat us when our love isn't big enough, when it doesn't give us the vision and passion to find solutions.

The needs of the soul, when considered together, can help us conceive and comprehend a love that is much more substantial and powerful than we currently think. Be very careful what you call love. Not everyone's love is worthy. What we need is love that generates growth, that frees us to be and do what we're created for, to be and do what is best for others and ourselves. In the light of this liberating love, we thrive. It drives out fear that controls us, stops us from effectively meeting our needs, and so prohibits our growth and development to realize self-actualizing transcendence.

The Bible has a chapter (1 Corinthians 13) articulating this essential, energizing quality. The first few verses express its value. Love gives meaning, significance, and relevance to great oration, profound knowledge, lofty confidence, and inspirational sacrifice. Without love, all those virtues amount to nothing. The middle passage lists its characteristics: patient, kind, content, humble, forgiving, magnanimous, evil-averse, truth-loving, always believing and hopeful, never-ending. The last third identifies its outcomes: fulfillment, maturity, clarity.

It is not love defined by any one of us, yet it is experienced and proven by healthy, long-lasting, committed relationships. It is genuine when the giver and receiver of this love grow in freedom and maturity.

It is evidenced by people who overcome fear-producing, false loves by uncovering hidden forces that kill inspiration and joy.

This love is an essential core of a broad and deep perspective. It is shaped by ideology where it is paramount, and trumps all other priorities, virtues, and values. As such, it guides and directs how and when we meet our needs—it is this divine gift that empowers us to overcome the conflicts of Erikson's stages of psychosocial development. This liberating energy leads us through levels of leadership consciousness from survival through transformation to vision and wisdom. Sun-sized love gives us visibility into what matters most and provides the energy to sustain healthy living. As a desire for the benefit and blessing of all people, it is the source of top level, profoundly meaningful goals. It is the inspiration for empowered relationships, dynamically motivating us with high levels of challenge and support. In turn, we engage others, especially our loved ones.

Does your perspective, your ideology, your theology, your philosophy, your worldview have this love integrally infused into it? I believe this love is the universal governing principle which sustains all of creation. It is the very heart and soul of the Creator.

History has shown us time and time again, at every level of society, from the family unit to the governance of the nation, this caliber of leadership moves the human race forward. It's about individuals at the right place and time, courageously choosing to respond to life's complexity, diversity, and preciousness rather than hold onto outdated, limiting rules and beliefs from culture and family of origin.

A great example is the movie *Hidden Figures*, which came out December 2016. It's the incredible story of Katherine G. Johnson, Dorothy Vaughan, and Mary Jackson, brilliant African-American women working at NASA in the '60s who excelled in their work while struggling against the bigotry of the times. The United States was falling behind in the Space Race against the Soviet Union, struggling with the task of putting a human being into orbit. Through talent, wisdom, and grace, the three women successfully navigated the challenges of prejudice and space travel, and significantly contributed to the advancement of technology in the United States, taking the lead by not only putting a man into orbit, but also on the moon.

Throughout the film, the line, "That's the way it is," is said by various characters. This attitude is indicative of a non-growth center and a mindset built on the foundation of fear. But the women didn't buy into that lie; they boldly embraced a vision of freedom, for that was truth. There's a moment halfway into the movie when Katherine Johnson asks to attend an editorial meeting about John Glenn's upcoming mission to become the first American to orbit the Earth. Head NASA engineer Paul Stafford refuses the request, saying, "There's no protocol for women attending." Johnson replied, "There's no protocol for a man circling Earth either, sir." It became quite evident that much of what was stopping NASA's progress in finding solutions was adherence to "protocol." Fortunately, the women had a bigger picture of life and work that surpassed most of their colleagues. "Each was uniquely aware of the broader stakes of their success—for other women, for black people, for black women, and for America at large."[10]

The needs for real solutions set the stage for the three heroines to change the world for the better. Because of her expertise in analytic geometry, Katherine is assigned to a special task group trying to get John Glenn into orbit. Glenn, a very real people person, is pivotal in NASA's culture shift away from prejudice and stifling ways of doing things. His unprejudiced care for everyone around him helps Katherine and NASA move forward in the organization's evolution toward equality and freedom.

Mary navigates layers of racist bureaucracy to become an engineer. Dorothy fights for a long overdue promotion as she faithfully manages the team of African-American women human computers. They are brilliant, fierce, and human. On weekends, they go to church and neighborhood barbecues. They spend time with their children. Their lives weren't perfect. How could it be, with such blatant racism? But they strove for balance and connection. Despite the environmental and cultural challenges Katherine, Dorothy, and Mary face, they prevail— not only because of their intelligence, but also what I sensed was their center. The movie doesn't "dwell much on the particulars of aeronautical science; instead, it revels in the intelligence and warmth of its subjects, in their successes both in and out of the office, and it wants viewers to do so too."[11] We see their genius at work, but we are

---

[10] Lenika Cruz, https://www.theatlantic.com/entertainment/archive/2017/01/hidden-figures-review/512252/

[11] Ibid

inspired by their love and humanity. Their humility, passion, and perseverance grounded them in their context and freed them from oppression.

Why do organizations (families, corporations, nonprofits, churches, companies, etc.) decline and die? No sun. Not enough gravitational force (love) to keep people around. Not enough light (truth, communication, honesty, authenticity) and heat (affection, encouragement, belonging). When you don't have enough of these, life-givingness is not sustained. Even if you have them, are they central and massive?

What exactly is the challenge? Non-massive centers include conformity, competition, fear, pragmatism, money, performance, and short-term priorities. These elements will never have what it takes to sustain a life-generating culture. They have their place, but when they become central, they corrupt. They cause willful blindness, resulting in widespread devastation of property and people's lives[12]. They cause us to close ourselves off to the healthy input of nutrients and elimination of waste. We become less and less humble to learn and explore, less honest to evaluate and examine—especially ourselves—and less courageous to eliminate what is unnecessary and toxic. Without emotional hygiene and moral courage, we lose out on relevant creativity and the innovation needed by the world around us, i.e. "market" needs and opportunities.

---

[12] Margaret Heffernan, *Willful Blindness*, 2011.

There was a lot of thought and wisdom that went into the design of our solar system. That's why it has lasted this long and why life is still around. If we want our organizations (family, company/corporation, nonprofit, church, etc.) to grow and sustain a culture that helps people thrive with increased quality of presence and productivity, we need to learn a few things from the Creator of the solar system and work according to a proven design.

This design is one where the environment of relationships is animated and energized by sun-like love. Every member is loved with commitment, resulting in the development of emotional and relational health and maturity—not only of the children, but also the parents. This means our definition and implementation of love prioritizes honest acknowledgement of feelings and needs for comfort, as well as the perceptions behind emotions that develop maturation. When you're immersed in this kind of culture, you discover better life balance and integration. You actively manage the hidden things creeping into our homes stealing time, driving emotional wedges, and polluting our perceptions of each other. You're less likely to neglect your soul and the souls of those you love. This intangible center is soul-thriving love. It produces liberating visibility and affections that empower everyone to benevolently lead and serve. This center prioritizes building up of what matters most—an identity rooted and functioning in love, wisdom, and legacy—for everyone. It eliminates elitism, dysfunctional invulnerability, and anything stifling essential freedoms (freedom of speech, freedom to express oneself, and freedom to seek new information). It's about learning to think and act with a developmental perspective that desires elevating equity for all.

In a growth-centered family, development is the primary dynamic priority—development of needs fulfillment, psychosocial maturation, and elevated consciousness. The parents—those responsible for leading and managing—think and act according to the requirements for positive, healthy human development. And it's this mindset which frees all members to grow and thrive. In this kind of culture, leaders operate from substantial, truthful, intimate knowledge of what matters most (souls, relationships, psychosocial direction and navigation). This happens through safe, trust-filled relationships. As time passes and things evolve, the leaders delegate and free themselves to focus on the most important priorities, giving from both their least and most effective talents—to give time, attention, and energy to growing what matters most.

This kind of culture endures because leaders are persistent, consistently communicating what matters most—the loving development of everyone in the organization (i.e. family, company, etc).

It all begins with your soul, the most important part of you. If your soul is healthy, it will write a story that makes courageous and compassionate sense of all the stuff that happens to you—even seemingly senseless pain, tragedies, and losses. We especially need a thriving soul in our most difficult relational areas—tensions with teens, midlife marriage mayhem, parent-caused pains, and atrophic aging anxieties.

Without a robust story writer, it's easy to come up with harmful perspectives and chaotic solutions that only make things worse. When our soul is not well, it dis-integrates. That means we are less and less connected to love that empowers and more controlled by fear and pessimism. Our narratives are depressing and hopeless, resulting in helplessness—"That's the way it is and there's nothing that can be done." We instinctively believe people don't, can't, and won't change, if we're not willing to work hard to cultivate inner life. We don't exercise courageous faith, and end up doing things the way they've always been done. This only perpetuates blindness to what's really needed for positive, innovative, world-changing ways of being and doing.

Wouldn't it be better to age with wisdom? To see yourself and others more clearly with love, making decisions redeeming the greatest value from all our heartache and craziness? When I think about the challenges of raising teens, midlife crises, aging, and dealing with elderly parents, it's a lack of psychological wisdom that causes failure. It's resisting the changes that sun-like love reveals. It's the stubborn attachment to outdated rules and limiting beliefs, resulting from insecurity, conformity and blind hubris.

Without a healthy soul, you will not be a secure connector, to weather life's storms and positively adapt to changes. If you don't do those things well, you will not have the life you really want. Whatever you build will get washed away because you did not build a solid foundation to bond you to those you love. Conversely, a healthy soul will help you ruthlessly eliminate haste, insecurity, blame, quick-temperedness, neglect of inner-life essentials, and toxic drives for secondary indicators of success—i.e. money and promotions.

When your soul is truly alive, you'll love yourself. When you love yourself, you'll love others with freedom rather than expectation and control. Howard Thurman famously said, "Don't ask what the world needs. Ask what makes you come alive, and go do it. Because what the world needs is people who have come alive." Soulfulness is doing things that help you...

- Believe you are indescribably precious.
- Rest in being fully loved.
- Indulge in your passion.
- Invest in your aspirations.
- Come alive and align your life with *your* purpose and dreams.

Increase your learning about soul- and self-care. Slow down to go farther, stronger, longer, and paradoxically faster. Create more time and space to love and be loved. Love enlivens our souls. We receive love through healing and transformation and then we share that love to others. When we fail—and we will—stick with your effort until fears and insecurities are undone. Dealing with emotional challenges is painful, but worth it. Without interior wellness, we will not love well. We may do a lot of things for those we love, but we will not be good at being with them in ways that truly build them up and draw us closer to each other.

Do our souls really need this kind of care? Well, when they're not healthy, disintegration occurs and eventually causes us to disconnect from who we really are and those we love most.

A thriving soul increases our emotional health. Without it, we won't manage conflict, fear, or loss. Controlled by our fight or flight responses, we avoid and hide or attack and destroy. With it, we'll stay connected and abide in conversations and relationships working toward mutual understanding and empathy, i.e. loving well. Developing these two areas is like a physical workout. You need a plan you'll stick with, to see results.

Plan for Patterns

What we do daily, weekly, monthly are the most powerful shapers for us as individuals and as families. Regular routines either integrate, or dis-integrate our souls. Just like food we put into our bodies, our activities and environments profoundly shape our view of the world, our ideologies, the sense we're making of all we see, hear, and experience. Healthy routines give us energy, strength, clarity, focus, and vital longevity. Conversely, bad habits and consistent exposure to dysfunction negatively impacts even diminishing our capacities to thrive and find meaningful fulfillment.

When your kids are adults, will they remember their childhood as a time of...

- Having fun together as a family?
- Being listened to?
- Being able to talk through difficult choices?
- Being encouraged and affirmed?
- Being valued for their unique personalities and gifts?
- Knowing and feeling they're loved?
- Learning important values, such as honesty and generosity?
- Learning to think about others as well as for themselves?
- Being prayed for?
- Having clear boundaries for their own protection?
- Seeing kindness modeled?

If your child experiences these, which needs (physiological, safety/security, love, belonging, self-esteem) are being met? The purpose of patterns is to create and sustain substantial soul fulfillment for all. We should not only want this for our kids, but for ourselves as well.

What does everyone in the family regularly do to help their souls thrive, positively navigate the various stage-specific conflicts and prepare for the next?

- Trust versus mistrust
- Autonomy versus shame and doubt
- Initiative versus guilt
- Industry versus inferiority
- Identity versus role confusion
- Intimacy versus isolation

- Generativity versus stagnation
- Integrity versus despair

We want our family life patterns to help all members overcome life stage challenges and prepare them for subsequent ones. Don't forget, as adults we need to keep growing in our identity and intimacy to move toward greater generativity and integrity. This involves dynamic, multifaceted strategies of healthy relationships, soul- and self-care, and management of time and other priorities.

Having a pattern implies a design with repetitive elements. Common family patterns are bedtime, dinnertime, fun time, downtime, as well as regular events like monthly movie nights, weekly grocery shopping, and getting together with extended family and friends. My son and I go fishing ten to fifteen times a year. I go to the movies with my daughter about the same number of times. I go shopping with my wife twelve to twenty times a year. The two of us also take walks two to four times a week. These patterns aren't static; they change through various life stages.

Creating patterns is a start, but the key is dynamically maintaining them—how we do so and what motivates us. It is simple to make a list of things to do and come up with a design. But the devil is in the details —mainly the detail of each person's enjoyment of the time and the sustainability of the activities. Thus, patterns need to be easy to implement, and this is directly correlated to frequency.

If planning is not really our thing, then we should adjust our expectations accordingly, and give ourselves time to learn and improve our skill. This is another reason to keep things going—to have the opportunity to identify obstacles and make changes. To do this effectively requires implementing and growing the other practices in this section, because they will orient and shape us to become people who will make these patterns enjoyable and sustainable.

Part Three and the appendix offer skills and tools to help you lead and manage your family patterns for a soulful center. They will help you cultivate preconditions empowering your family to scale up in unique, beautiful ways. I hope that your patterns foster fulfillment of all needs and you both see and experience the satisfaction and joy of every member's development and maturation.

For starters, carve a few minutes each day to slow down and be still. Find a time and place to sit, relax, close your eyes, and focus on your breathing. If your thoughts rush off to your task list, let them. But intentionally bring your thinking back to focus on your breath and the sensations of your body and be present in this moment. (Download the app 'Headspace'; it's an easy guide to growing this activity).

If you're a person of faith, pray. Give attention to your feelings, your emotional climate, i.e. your general mood and self talk. Acknowledge God and His place in your life, open yourself to His will for forgiveness, growth, and freedom. Ask for His healing leadership, empowerment for grace and truth to overcome inner strongholds resisting transformation and emotional maturity.

Developing a consistent practice of intentional pausing, slowing down, managing thoughts, processing desires and knowing feelings encourages us to care for our souls. As our internal wellness and maturity progresses, we invigorate our relationships. This becomes a culture continually shaping our families with greater levels of overall balance, fitness, and aspirations. When this center is substantial and massive, we find the love, clarity, courage, and compassion for leading our families with revolutionary authenticity. We learn and change to be present and productive in ways that both challenge and support soulful living.

Chapter 9: Freed by Transformation

A family centered on growth is passionate about freedom. The passion comes from a heart enlivened by radical beliefs in sun-like love and soul caring practice. The freedom is born from struggle and victory against cultural, historical (i.e. family of origin) expectations, rules, and beliefs that are no longer relevant or effective. It leaves a life centered on things ineffective against fear. It grows a life centered on creating and cultivating our truest and best identity—one enabling us to continue maturing as adults, producing the integrity our families need for continuous thriving.

This freedom results from deep transformation of one's organizing principle, i.e. letting go of scarcity mindedness in order to embrace sufficiency. If we default to a sense of scarcity, we operate from a place of insecurity and deficiency. We do not treat either others or ourselves with high levels of honor and honesty. Scarcity tells us there's never enough, and outcomes must always have a winner and loser. Scarcity does not have the insight and courage to explore new ways of being and unconventional resources and methods. It blinds us to our own potential.

What beliefs lie at the root of our scarcity stories? Lynne Twist calls them "Mythic Themes of Scarcity."[13] They are propagated by cultures, families, and individuals.

- "There's not enough."
- "More is always better."
- "That's just the way it is and always will be."

---

[13] Lynne Twist, *The Soul of Money*, 2003.

Even the Bible's narrative about sin's origin involves the first man and woman falling into temptation because they were offered a lie, inducing a sense of not being enough. In Genesis 3:5, the serpent said, "Your eyes will be open and you will be like God, knowing good and evil," implying they didn't see enough, that they were not enough like God. After ingesting the deception, they felt shame—the essence of the lie of scarcity—and they sought to cover themselves. Now, multiply and compound that by millennia of generations and we have the mythic themes firmly rooted in our culture, even in our DNA.

When these themes are adopted and become code in our operating system (our soul), we experience dysphoric outcomes: insecurity, discouragement, dysfunctional management of pain, fear, and shame. The end is corruption and despair. Embedded senses of deficit generate ongoing, inner chatter, feelings hindering learning and becoming emotionally and relationally mature. Unexamined beliefs and rules lodge in our gut, often outside our consciousness, and sabotage the development of wisdom and creativity. These compel us to sacrifice our hearts and others', destroying our relationships. In extreme cases, even acts of dehumanization occur to secure one's own prosperity and security. Insecurity, anxiety, and panic drive decisions and behaviors prioritizing busyness, performance, achievement, acquiring—all in the pursuit of security and success. These actions break down relationships, both at work and at home. Spouses lose intimacy and trust. Parents and kids get disconnected, with everyone 'doing their own thing'. Work becomes a beast that devours years of life, causing neglect of the most important things for personal success and fulfillment—faith, love of and for family and friends, overall fitness, and healthy management of finances.

In stark contrast, sufficiency believes there is always enough. Twist explains, "It is an experience, a context we generate, a declaration, a knowing that there is enough, and that we are enough…. It is a consciousness, an attention, an intentional choosing of the way we think about our circumstances…. Sufficiency is an act of generating, distinguishing, making known to ourselves the power and presence of our existing resources, and our inner resources…. When we live in the context of sufficiency, we find a natural freedom and integrity. We engage in life from a sense of our own wholeness rather than a desperate longing to be complete."[14] At the core, sufficiency believes "there is always enough," "less can be better," and "things can change/I can change." This is the profound, freeing effect of having a healthy soul. It increases our awareness of what's available and possible. It vastly improves our attitudes and grows our ability to change our perspective, our circumstances, and our lives.

Transformational freedom is about shifting from a mindset of scarcity to one of sufficiency—replacing the harmful myths with life-giving certainty. It's going from being fear-based to faith-based, freeing us to take advantage of more opportunities for learning, enrichment, and empowerment. To move from cowardice to courage, to do what is needed when no one else will or can. Insecurity to assurance. Apathy to passion. False control to real freedom. It's about surrendering to the

---

[14] Lynne Twist, The Soul of Money, p.73-74, 2003.

power of vulnerability and love—the source of healthy, sustainable growth and thriving.

It starts with vulnerability—being open to needs, possibilities, limitations, challenges, failures, joy, pain, peace, chaos, fear, and even eternal life and love—all of it. This is the tapestry of authentic human life. When we close ourselves off to any of it, our souls experience disintegration, and we lose capacity to love and thrive. Openness comes from courageous choices, but it also generates courage to believe in the omnipotence of love to win over all, to redeem anything, to transform everything—beginning with ourselves. Surrendering to this truth radically alters our stories, frees our passions and values by profound, powerful fulfillment of deep needs.

This liberty doesn't come naturally. It's actually unnatural, even supernatural, and comes only through radical transformation. It's freeing the soul from a base of fear to one of love. Significant, authentic transformation won't come through drifting, driving, or quick fixes—all symptoms of restlessness. It comes through a rested soul. And out of this fortified core, humility, clarity, creativity, wholehearted desire, perseverance, and openness to accountability can flow to grow a sustainable life of health and vitality, which is a growth-centered family.

Where might we begin? Dallas Willard prescribed, "Ruthlessly eliminate hurry." We'd do well to apply this to our daily schedule, as well as our shorter- and longer-term goals and objectives. Why? Because to impact and change our core, we need a restful structure to effectively think and deal with the instinctual myths that control our narratives and emotions, which directly affect how we manage our relationships, resources, and time. Just how important is this need for rest? The Bible (Hebrews 4:11) puts it this way, "Let us, therefore, make every effort to enter that rest, so that no one will perish by following their example of disobedience." The disobedience refers to the nation of Israel's refusal to enter God's rest, the Promised Land. It's important to note that it was a nation's refusal; the substantial cultural influence of large groups of people that are indoctrinated with the "not enough" philosophy will invariably make it incredibly difficult to enter a life of soulful rest and liberty. 'Everyone is doing it' is one of the firmest oppositions to finding rest for our souls.

Larger, highly-populated societies and cultures impact the smaller-scale context of families—the shaping place. We are all radically impacted and influenced by those who raised us. This segment of our history is a big part of who we are and determines, to some extent, the rest of our lives. Our stories (shaped by environments and perceptions) determine how we prioritize and manage our time and resources. Sustained over long periods of time, our stories, actions, and behaviors create cultures. Culture creation is unavoidable; we are both creators and the affected. If we are from restrictive cultures, we've likely developed apathy, low expectations, entitlement, mistrust, fear, and manipulation. If we've lived in cultures that challenged and supported us, we likely developed empowerment and opportunity.

But there is countercultural wisdom, and Dallas Willard offers a counterintuitive strategy. "Ruthlessly eliminate hurry. Substantially slow down. Our souls desperately need it." If you've started a practice of meditation and/or prayer, slow down some more to dream and envision what you want your life to be in the long term. Create a list of goals related to the 5 Fs of a fulfilled life: Faith, Family, Friends, Fitness, and Finances (contributed by James Hansberger, a longtime wealth manager for Morgan Stanley). We can use the 5 F's to shape our dreams and evaluate the joy factor when managing our daily activities and short-term objectives (ninety days, six months, twelve months). Do they line up with the most meaningful, top-level goals? Don't rush this development. As your soul is strengthened and what matters most is clarified, your organizing principle will become more and more evident. And as this occurs, continue to ruthlessly eliminate things that do not move you forward toward sufficiency. The outcome of this exercise should reveal how less can be more, and this liberates us to focus on prioritizing what matters most.

In Mark 8:36, Jesus says, "For what does it profit a man to gain the whole world yet forfeit his soul?" He wasn't simply referring to the afterlife. He was pointing to the invaluable worth of the inner life for health and happiness. This inner life must not be denied or sacrificed. Neglecting it always results in unhealthy relationships decreasing our ability to achieve sustainable success. Forfeit the soul and we're stuck in dysfunction and despair, suffering cancers of conformity, collusion, and corruption. Gaining or maintaining the world at the expense of our soul is a common, human failure.

To be the leaders of their families and builders of their homes, parents must have a substantial foundation of fulfilled needs, from physiological to self-worth. To thrive as parents, we've got to know and act according to who we really are, not who our parents and cultures tell us to be. Why is this critical? Effective leadership and management depend on accurate assessment and understanding of the dynamic conditions of the company and the market. The need for true knowledge is even greater for family members. Our parents may have no clue as to what's going on in our families, and neither does the culture or society at large. Most often, their observations are superficial and speculative. An even greater consideration is whether parents individuated successfully. If not, why would we let them govern how we raise our kids? We can value their input, but with no obligation to implement it.

Richard Barrett[15] identifies a critical stage in the evolution of human consciousness: individuation. Here we learn to let go of parental and cultural expectations preventing our maturation. Here an individual transforms by letting go of outdated rules and limiting beliefs. Without this foundational freedom, not only do we struggle intensely as parents, but we miss out on living our true purpose and leading a values driven life. We don't find alignment and collaboration with others of like mind and heart to maximize our impact in the world. The world and more importantly, our families, will miss a legacy-building culture where we can share our greatest gifts and strengths of love and courage.

Personal transformation is not an event, but an essential part of lifelong progress and maturation. It marks the transition from the three lower levels of psychological development to the three higher ones (see

---

[15] https://www.valuescentre.com/sites/default/files/uploads/
The_Seven_Stages_of_Psychological_Development.pdf

graphic). When this process works, it adds continuous renewal and growth that empower us to change, adapt, lead, and manage according to our 'season of life'. We become connected to our souls, to others, and to God. This enhances how we meet all our needs, overcome challenges of psychosocial stages, and move toward greater levels of sustainable, healthy leadership. Most importantly, this process helps us maximize our potential to create the most meaningful life possible.

Transformation is not only mental and emotional work, but also the result of changes in time management, our decisions about what's real and important, and our ability to lead during difficulties. It places our confidence in real strength, rather than counterfeits. Above all, transformation grounds us in commitment to values, thoughts, and actions that prioritize healthy development. It connects us with each other and the world to collaborate in redemptive evolution that makes sense of all of human history, even our own stories.

How does all this happen? As you allow yourself to be vulnerable and get clearer about what matters most to you, you grow greater awareness of your path to action—your emotions, stories you tell yourself, and your interpretation of data. Then, you recruit all minds— head, heart, and gut—to align with your essential wants arranging your days to impact will, mind, and body through consistent, healthy, empowering habits and routines.

Getting vulnerable, clarifying and aligning your three "minds" helps you better fulfill your needs, in turn freeing you to increasingly embody your values. This empowers you to make life-changing choices, opening up a world of possibilities to create the life and environment you truly want for your family and yourself. No longer bound by one, hard-pressed choice, you find freedom to explore, learn, change, shapeshift, transform.

On top of this, you improve your ability to problem solve, especially with critical life issues, e.g.., dynamically fulfilling your vows, successfully raising your kids, directing your life choices, positively influencing your family, impacting the world with your gifts and strengths. All this has the potential to revolutionize society, culture, and power structures toward healthier, more meaningful dynamics to everyone's benefit.

Transformation launches you into a life of continuous learning, renewal, and improvement—healthy, sustainable, positive growth. We need freedom from the default of always looking for people like ourselves. Only then do we embrace diversity to authentically collaborate in overcoming the difficulties of larger-scale challenges like cultural dysfunctions.

Lastly, transformation elevates your commitment to your most important goals. The increased vitality of your soul, the deeper connections with loved ones, greater internal cohesion and external collaboration, take your grit to new levels. Not only do you persevere with more endurance, but your pace and clarity enable you to see needed course corrections sooner, making your execution that much more effective. What will this look like in the life of your family? You are dynamically present for your spouse and children during each stage of development, from diapers to toddlerhood, separation anxieties to adolescent attitudes. As parents, we move from young adulthood to older adulthood, from intimacy to generativity and integrity. Our loved ones need us to be committed to them through all the joys and pains of growth. With passing years, and changing family needs, our leadership and management grows in complexity. Successful commitment requires flexibility, courage, grace, and wisdom.

Transformation empowers us to be present to meet the needs of our loved ones. It protects us from the chaos and harm occurring when needs are not being met or met ineffectively. When our consciousness is no longer obsessed with meeting basic needs, futilely doing so with false assets, we are free as the visionary servant leaders our families need us to be.

You want transformation in your life. If you don't have experience in this area, it's time to learn. Give attention to pain—any pain, physical, emotional, relational, organizational. Take time to find its root; stop denying, neglecting, avoiding, medicating, or distracting. Stop choosing not to know. If you feel like your identity has a sinkhole in its foundation, courageously assess, inspect, and seek help to learn and grow. Take the bold step.

Fear and insecurity keep us doing the same things. What encourages us to step off the hamster wheel? We need to know that whatever happens, things will turn out well in the end. We need something to drive out fear of failure and the confidence to always get back up and try again—try something new, learn and improve. Finding the best solutions—this is what deep change is all about.

Transformation makes us people who discover and create juggernaut goals—not only the ends, but the means as well. Transformation pulls us off the conformity track to become creators. It's about seeing in better ways to find greater inspiration, innovation, and implementation to adapt and take advantage of opportunities. Moreover, it empowers us to increase the purity and wisdom of our trust and love, providing an unstoppable vision of two radical categories:

1.The kind of person you want to be—core values and beliefs that align your ideologies, mental models, and worldviews.

2.The kind of life you want to live—living from that core to achieve fulfillment and success consistent with your ideologies, mental models, and worldviews.

What would these juggernauts do for you and your family/organization? They let you know that whatever happens, you're still going to achieve what matters most in the long run. This level of confidence comes from a healthy soul, gut, and heart; it's not simply thinking something. It's daily creating spaciousness for patience and courage. This maintains openness for change and readiness for future possibilities. The opposite—less lofty goals—close off options, frustrate, compromise relationships, health, ultimately destroying hope for what you really want.

Juggernaut end-goals can come to us when we slow down (voluntarily or involuntarily) and stop adrenaline drive and unceasing analysis. They require wisdom to navigate the complexities and challenges that come with the adventure of prioritizing the hard work of relationships and emotional maturation. Achieving all-powerful end goals requires deep revolution from common cultural norms creating exhausting competition for opportunities or resources. This means making brave, difficult choices.

Eliminating hurry shows we are learning and applying this counterintuitive truth and proactively pursuing freedom. In the 2015 Willow Creek Global Leadership Summit, Bill Hybels (Senior Pastor of Willow Creek Community Church) interviewed Ed Catmull (CEO of Pixar Studios) about creating a sustainable culture of creativity. At the close of the session, both men talked about the importance of getting away from everything periodically (at least every four to five days) to clear their minds of chatter and allow their hearts to open to the stillness, reminding them they are not the chatter, but eternal souls— loved and cherished apart from performance and productivity. They both affirmed the need to care for this most important part of themselves.

Create space and time for soul care. Take on the role of gardener in your family, as well as your own life. Renew your mind. Recreate your environment and structure. Reinvigorate your relationships. Reframe life as one grounded in sufficiency, not scarcity. Transform your perceptions with courageous candor, healthy compassion, benevolent operations, creative problem solving, and executive processing to organize deeper issues and achieve loftier goals. If we don't make time for inner restoration and change, we must expect the opposite—disintegration due to others' expectations, pressures of performance and productivity, limiting beliefs, and outdated rules. We will likely live out our days perpetually trying to solve problems with the same mindset that caused them initially. Our most precious connections diminish as we continue to behave in fearful, insecure ways. We miss out on growing a community of maturity, legacy, and integrity that only comes through transformation.

As you continue on freedom's path, overcoming the challenges of inner life revolution, your soul becomes stronger in its connectivity—to God, others, and yourself. Connections are threatened every time conflict occurs. Hurt feelings, stress attacks, broken trust, harsh words, overwhelming fear strikes us. Many families suffer and disintegrate because they lack securing attitudes and the ability to communicate candidly and safely. Becoming grounded, even rooted, in sufficiency is the source of secure connection to others. Milan and Kay Yerkovich[16] summarize secure connection this way:

- I have a wide range of emotions and express them appropriately.
- It is easy for me to ask for help and receive from others when I have needs.
  - I can say "no" to others even when I know it will upset them.
  - I'm adventuresome and I know how to play and have fun.
I know I'm not perfect, and I give my loved ones room to disagree.

---

[16] https://www.howwelove.com/love-styles/

Being like this is not only secure, but also refreshing and renewing. Transformative. Liberating. These qualities and skills are essential for healthy parenting, and basically any form of management. If we've been blessed by these secure connectors, it's likely we've become a mature, balanced adult, able to figure out the healthy leadership puzzle. If we do not possess the understanding and competence to navigate emotionally difficult situations, it's likely we are not free from immature or scarcity-based models of reality (M.O.R.).

An M.O.R. is constructed by beliefs and values formulating rules for choices, shaping attitudes, and determining responses. It may not be the same as ideology of philosophy for living. It's a subconscious, default framework shaping our perceptions and causing our knee-jerk reactions. It's another capacity of the soul, in addition to story writing. Our M.O.R. forms in youth and becomes our subconscious operating system, running in the background—integrating all data and experiences to generate a "big picture".

In adolescence, our M.O.R. must go through radical reorganization, a metamorphosis replacing a child's model with an adult's. Ideally, this reflects the uniqueness of the individual with   support and challenge of emotionally healthy parents. This can easily not be the case. If Mom and Dad do not have a center to foster healthy inner life, factors may negatively affect adolescent outcomes.

If we aren't freed, we have not experienced transformation. We aren't being transformed because we are not changing how we think or act. We're not changing because we aren't ruthlessly eliminating hurry. We aren't eliminating hurry because we're likely operating on restlessness caused by enslavement to scarcity. Without an unhurried life, we can't practice self-reflexivity[17], the capacity for metacognition (stepping back to reflect on self and thought processes). We need to be able to think deeply about who we are, what we are, where we're heading, and the M.O.R.s driving it all.

What's your model of reality and its beliefs, the unconscious views driving responses to pain, stress, fear, and struggle?

Here are examples of default, instinctual beliefs:
- I am worthy of love and acceptance only when I get what I want.
- I am worthy of love and acceptance only when I'm perfect.
- I am worthy only when I achieve great success.
- I am happy and secure only when I am financially wealthy.
- I am hated and being humiliated when others disagree with me or reject my ideas.

You can pretty easily imagine the corresponding behaviors. If the belief is, "I am worthy of love and acceptance only when I get what I want," then the rule is, "If I get what I want, I have value." Or, if it's "I am worthy only when I'm perfect," then the commandment will be, "Strive for perfection at all costs." These beliefs are unintentionally created by well-intentioned parents and cultures driven by imbalanced priorities.

---

[17] Marilyn Mandala Schlitz, Cassandra Vieten, Tina Amorok, *Living Deeply: The Art and Science of Transformation in Everyday Life*, 2008.

They are seldom explicit, but operate in the background and are revealed by how we resolve conflict, how we care for ourselves, and how we manage our time and resources.

What outcomes do these rules and behaviors produce? Boundaries are unhealthy, as satisfaction is pursued at the cost of one's own and others' wellbeing. There's nothing wrong with caring for oneself or pursuing perfection, but when it's tied to our sense of worth, limits that sustain us and our relationships are easily neglected. Then, health suffers.

How do you know if your M.O.R. needs updating? Here are somethings that are telling us it's time:
- We're stuck in unhealthy behaviors, patterns, and relationships
- Our decisions are more fear-based than love-based.
- We struggle to manage our emotions.
- We're not changing, evolving, and maturing in the numerous balance areas of life. (love, relationships, friendships, adventures, environment, health and fitness, intellectual life, skills, spiritual life, career/business, creativity, family life, and community life)

Indicators aren't limited to negative ones. Perhaps we are experiencing these:
- We want more love, joy, peace, and hope.
- We want more freedom to be and do our best at home and at work.
- We want to tackle life's complexity and grow meaning, happiness, and success.

It's common to operate from outdated codes written in us without our being conscious of them. It's also common to accept them, allowiung them to dictate without challenge. And if we're distracted by things like fear, fatigue, insecurities, and just plain old busyness, we may not have taken time to evaluate and update these rules. We've unknowingly been loyal to that which prevents us from moving forward.

So, once we've spotted some of our **obsolete orders**, what then? First, understand where they come from:

- Authority figures, i.e. parents, teachers, elders
- Culture, i.e. gender roles, definition of success
- Media portrayals of strength, security, and significance

These sources usually mean well but their rules get embedded early in our lives for good, bad or both. Over time, they are deeply rooted if we don't test, evaluate, and decide for ourselves whether or not we want to follow them.

It's also possible we developed them in response to stressful periods of time when we regularly lived with anxiety, fear, failure, and /or pain. Being controlled by default codes results from longstanding patterns and experiences. Getting rid of them (updating our OS) involves doing things that don't feel normal; it is uncomfortable, to say the least. It can feel like persecution, as you stand for something new and different.

But if we're serious about authentic growth, transformation, and healthy maturation, sticking with the process of replacing our rules liberates us to greater levels of freedom, joy, and wellness. So here are twelve things that may help you discover and update your operating system:

1.Retreats, with more rest/sleep

2.Improved diet and fitness

3.Meditation

4.Faking it till you make it

5.Being a part of a new family/community

6.Moving/relocating

7.Changing career

8.Counseling/coaching

9.Breaking away from unhealthy people

10.Education

11.Recreation

12.Transformative programs, such as recovery and/or leadership development

It's not necessarily the activity, but your engagement with your default M.O.R.—being aware of its negative control, struggling with its rooted resistance, and overthrowing them—that the activity creates. Keep in mind, it's common for rules to be embedded for lengthy periods of time. It's not a quick fix to break free and replace them with new code; in other words, plan for a process not days or weeks long, but rather months and maybe years. It's not going to be easy, but it's definitely worth it.

Replacing your outmoded decrees and updating your model is fundamental to improving the quality of your future—personally and professionally—and most importantly the future of your family. Neglect it, and your wellness, performance, impact, contributions, and influence will suffer.

To transform the code level of our lives, we need to talk to ourselves *through what we do*. For example, If we sit all day, we're telling our body we don't need muscle. Consistently skipping meals and eating tiny portions will tell our metabolism to slow down. Choose to be alone, and we tell our heart it doesn't need love. If we're always busy, we tell our soul it doesn't matter. You get the idea.

It's important to connect our actions with outcomes we really want, whether at work or home, in our projects or relationships. An example of a great action that sends a powerful message to our bodies: strength training. Resistance exercises involving multiple joints—squatting with weights—put a load on the entire musculoskeletal system. It tells the body, "Produce testosterone. We need more muscle!"

But let's not stop there. Let's apply it to tell our hearts and souls a message like, "Produce more love by building more life-generating trust." What might be the multiple-joint exercise that puts a load on our entire psycho-emotional-spiritual system? What can we regularly do that will recruit mind, soul, heart, and body?

●Make time to enjoy each other.

●Commit to ample rest; prioritize it.

●Grow deep mutual trust by exercising vulnerability, courage, compassion, and empathy.

●Forgive and be forgiven.

When we consistently do these, our entire being gets the message to pursue more of what's most important. Take time to get clear, update, and develop your M.O.R. for richer relationships, greater joy with those you love. Discover higher levels of health in balanced areas of life. Commit to regularly investing in what matters most by doing things to grow and fortify your M.O.R.

Freedom is the greatest measure of true love, and we need M.O.R.'s that enable true liberty. Love is genuine and from above when it results in freedom for both the lover and the one being loved. Freedom from things that enslave and oppress. Freedom to become mature. What does this freedom look like? Here's a great list[18]:

- Free to ask for what I need—comfort, intimacy, forgiveness, mercy—clearly, directly, honestly.
- Free to recognize, manage, and take responsibility for my thoughts and feelings.
- Free under stress to express my own beliefs and values without being adversarial.
- Free to respect others without having to change them.
- Free to give people room to make mistakes and learn from them.
- Free to appreciate people for who they are—the good, bad, and ugly.

---

[18] Peter Scazzero, *Emotionally Healthy* Spirituality, 2014.

•Free to assess my own limits, strengths, and weaknesses and discuss them with others.

•Free to be in tune with my emotional world and able to enter into the feelings, needs, and concerns of others without losing myself.

•Free to resolve conflict maturely and negotiate solutions that consider the perspective of others.

If we're truly loving ourselves and others, we grow those freedoms. How free are you? What will you do to tell yourself you're deeply loved in order to better love others? What will you stop doing to let yourself know that you're not hated and that a thriving you is desired for the long haul?

Could this be a primary reason why people in power lose sight of what's most important? Why they make decisions that neglect long-term welfare for themselves, those they serve, and even their families? They've lost connection with their own souls, and thus have no capacity to meaningfully connect with others. Without such connection, conformity, competition, and collusion cause gradual blindness to the value of human life and the necessary relationships to validate it. In that milieu, individuals and families get sacrificed for business needs and success. This is historically common, yet tragic.

In contrast, transformed people with new M.O.R.s make brave and compassionate decisions liberating families and organizations to greater levels of wellness and mutual success. They create cultures of empowerment and opportunity for everyone to thrive.

This chapter discussed transformation as an essential key to being a growth-centered family. I encourage you to pursue transformation, for the sake of your soul and your family. Part Three of this book shares more activities and tools to help you go deeper into the process. If they're new to you, I hope they spur you toward radical renewal. If they're familiar, I pray for greater immersion in the way, truth, and life that is truly abundant.

Chapter 10: Liberated Leaders

"Leadership is about making others better as a result of your presence and making sure that impact lasts in your absence." Sheryl Sandberg, Facebook COO

With a soul-fulfilling center, we are transforming. Being transformed, we are freed to really make a difference. Making positive, substantial impact is a high-level motivation of authentic leadership. When it comes to our families, we want to make a difference in their lives by giving them the best—not something we can buy or achieve through financial success, but rather the kind of spouse and parent we become. How amazing would it be for parents to lead in ways that empower and liberate all family members for success and fulfillment that continues to bless in their absence? Let's look again at the psychosocial development stages to get a better idea of what "the best" is: trust, autonomy, initiative, industry, identity, intimacy, generativity, and integrity.

A growth-centered family is a team with leaders who cultivate all eight presence-improving qualities. In so doing, they liberate themselves and their children from cultural and familial dysfunctions. They're protected from unhealthy conformity and pressures from others whose souls are mired in scarcity rather than sufficiency. They prioritize being authentically present. Giving more weight to productivity than presence significantly creates unhealthy conformity and blindness; turning that upside down helps lead us toward the awesome, innovative, renewable potential that come through growth-centered presence.

Again, consider Heffernan's powerful, historical examples of unhealthy conformities and pressure[19]—devastating tragedies of widespread sexual child abuse (Catholic diocese in Ireland during the late twentieth century), national financial corruption in the 2000's, x-raying pregnant women for over a quarter century in the 1900's. These incidents of willful blindness started as insecure affinities that degenerated into calamities, collusion, and cover-ups. These are the disastrous costs of masses unsuccessfully confronting challenges of psychosocial stages to become people who prioritize intimacy, generativity, and integrity. Their perspectives became toxic and narrow, steeped in fear-driven decisions, defaults, and deeds. We need leaders who overcome this profound danger, people who steer us toward transforming priorities.

How well do you know your presence? Steve Cockram and Jeremie Kubicek, Giant Worldwide co-founders, give us these eight questions we can't ignore if we want to be effective leaders:

1. Do you know what it's like to be on the other side of you?

2. Do you know how to connect with people in every social context?

3. Are you easy to connect with in your work setting?

4. Do people like being around you?

5. Are you able to be physically and emotionally present with people even when you have tight deadlines?

6. Do you always have to win?

---

[19] Margaret Heffernan, *Willful Blindness*, 2011.

7. Have you truly ever experienced being present with someone else?

8. Do you know how to slow down enough to hear what someone else is saying?

If you answer these negatively, you may lack awareness of where, when, and how you are disconnected. Does your stress response fill your mind and body with discomfort, discouragement, and soul fatigue? Did past hurts induce detachment from your emotions, leading to depression? Whatever the cause, resultingly we find it more and more difficult to enjoy our kids and spouse. We're not motivated to support and develop our direct reports. We don't effectively engage our peers on the executive board. We try to make ourselves invulnerable, increasing self-protection, avoiding pain by numbing ourselves with overworking, overeating, abusing our minds and bodies by disregarding limits and health needs. These behaviors kill us. When confronted, we withdraw, make excuses, or become hostile. We may try to change, but with little success. We give up.

To thrive, we've got to adopt what Brene Brown calls the power of vulnerability. It's counterintuitively powerful, but when this kind of change happens in tough places, amazing and miraculous things happen. Long-term relationships are rich with opportunities, purpose, and profound depth of meaning. Cockram and Kubicek state that the ability to be authentically present with high levels of emotional health is the "future competitive advantage for leaders."

This is not only for those naturally strong in relationships. It's something everyone should master. It is getting clearer that in the current work climate it's no longer about doing more, but rather leading more. And to lead, we must be able to influence through presence, not production. This is most true at home with our loved ones. Often, there's way too much being done for each other and way too little of creating a growth-centered environment by being truly present with emotional health and maturity. While there's nothing wrong with serving each other, it is much less significant than what we're like when we move together. This is most critical when tension mounts. We disagree. We are annoyed with each other. Our patience and tolerance runs out. We're hungry, anxious, lonely, or just tired. The atmosphere we create and bring with us may be invisible, but becomes quite palpable. An emotionally healthy presence cannot be overlooked. It creates sustainable environments and cultures. It's non-negotiable if we want to last.

What's the presence in your home? Is it two-dimensional, 3D, or 4D?

- 2D = Left brain; life is about doing. Productivity is usually high.
- 3D = Left + right brains engaged; life is about getting things done and fulfilling relationships. There is both productivity and presence experienced and enjoyed.
- 4D = Left + right brains + heart brain + gut brain; life is about all the above, but also elevating integration of identity, purpose, and story with another's inner dynamics to find greater solutions to change their relationship and world.

Four-dimensional presence is created by leaders who have matured to the point of seeing vulnerability and surrender as strengths empowering them to take on and truly value the perspective of another.[20] In so doing, they fulfill a need of their inner lives—to feel understood and have their thoughts and feelings validated. This is a great synthesis of previous chapters in this section. 4D leading is aligning with the universe by becoming developed and seasoned in sun-like liberating love, managing one's emotions and relationships well, and overcoming hidden forces stalling and diminishing fulfillment and success.

In our homes, 2D and 3D leadership may create success and happiness. But only 4D leadership will create transformative legacies. Why transformative? Due to the immaturity and dysfunction we all have (we all grew up with it) continually getting in the way of loving well, and is most poignant in spousal and parent-child relationships. Whether at home or in organizations, these invisible inhibitors keep us stuck or worse. The root of it all is in our families of origin and the cultures that fostered beliefs, rules, and values that are outdated and limiting. What would happen if we all break free from this age-old challenge? We become life-giving parents who raise new generations with wisdom, innovation, and discipline to bring the profound changes our world desperately needs.

4D leadership upgrades one's operating systems—our souls. Alan Watkins, in his book, *4D Leadership: Competitive Advantage*

---

[20] Alan Watkins, *4D Leadership: Competitive Advantage Through Vertical Leadership Development* 1st Edition, 2015.

Through Vertical Leadership Development, describes it as increasing the sophistication of doing, being, and relating—taking them to another level. It's adding the dimension of deeper integration to keep what matters most up front and center. It's giving greatest priority to interior life, resulting in elevation of other, external dimensions. This is much needed in our current environments, where change is constant and must be embraced and leveraged to find greater solutions—solutions that change the world but do not sacrifice what is most precious—our families.

Steve and Jeremie go so far as to say, "In the new world, the capacity to establish, develop, and maintain key relationships both inside and outside your organization is going to become the primary currency of leadership influence."

What level of leader are you at home? What's your capacity to establish, develop, and maintain your key life relationships, especially as your loved ones age? I'd like to apply Robert Hargrove's model[21] to the family to help us get clearer about our needs for effective leadership:

- Level 1: Are you a highly capable individual with 10,000-plus hours of mastery? This means being around and performing the many duties of a parent. You're responsible and you know your family members well.

---

[21] http://www.roberthargrove.com/seven-levels-of-leadership/

- Level 2: Do you multiply growth and benefits for your loved ones? This involves doing less for them and more development so that they can "catch their own fish."

- Level 3: Are you a continuous improver of life for those who matter most to you? This is about leading by balancing various areas of life so that overall fitness is not compromised (emotional, physical, spiritual, career, environment, lifestyle, vision, etc.).

- Level 4: Do you accelerate strategic execution as your marriage and kids grow? This is being able to shift focus and priorities as you and your spouse age, your marriage evolves, and your children are increasingly independent.

- Level 5: Are you an accelerating strategic aligner for your family members' development? This is an evolution from Level 4 to becoming more and more of a supportive facilitator of each member's maturation, which may include their young families, along with your own.

- Level 6: Are you a visionary, game-changing outperformer when it comes to the things that matter most? Keeping the main thing—sun-like love—alive with passion, practice, purpose, and hope as everyone ages.

- Level 7: Most importantly, are you changing the course of your family's history? Do you persevere, seeing your strategy's effect and success with desirable outcomes beyond what you imagined!

10,000 hours equates to about five work years, just about the time a child is off to kindergarten. As children progress through the six elementary years (K-fifth), parents do well to develop their leadership from project team leader to becoming a great leader. That's what kids truly need as they embark on the journey of adolescence. Our children want and need great leadership from their moms and dads, not just someone who manages things the kids should grow to manage themselves.

When the slippery slopes of the teenage conflict years arrive, it's time for accelerated strategic execution and alignment. If we want to be the best parents during the six or seven short years of adolescence, we need to lead with bravery, influence, and clarity. These years are colored by leaving secure childhood and heading toward the unknowns of being an adult. Teens are at a unique, profound place of substantial transformation, and need to be given space to learn to successfully lead and manage themselves. We need to align with where they're at, rather than trying to make them conform to our expectations. We need to ask questions, listen well, and reflect on their challenges in loving ways that will keep their learning channels open. We want them to be free to make mistakes. More importantly, we want them to learn from mistakes and exercise leadership and management of their own lives. We need to execute this strategy and align with our children's ongoing development if we want them to become great decision makers. The more we coddle them, make choices for them, protect them from mistakes and failures, the less they will practice leading and learning.

Imagine the incredible support your teens could have when they're connected to a visionary game changer, a parent who applies their primary passion and focus to cultivating unconventional, innovative, life-giving relationships with them, rather than pouring it all into work—benefitting their organizations and companies, but giving leftovers to those most precious to them.

Level 7 leadership can be elusive. Much of human history is repetitive because we don't learn from it. We need to have a clear understanding of what drove our ancestors to do what they did if we want to meaningfully alter the course of history. Providing a nicer lifestyle is a common pursuit, and it is one facet of course change. Success at work can be satisfying in the short term, but if emotional and relational health is sacrificed, compromised, or neglected, history is repeated. Age-old ways of managing conflict and negative emotions remain the same—namely, using performance, activity, productivity, tangible possessions, control, manipulation, and oppression to pursue peace and happiness rather than doing the much more significant work of interior life growth. Great leaders alter the course. The greatest leader, Jesus Christ, put it this way: "What does it profit to gain the whole world but lose your soul?"

Successful execution depends on how we lead ourselves. Are we leading ourselves and families toward integration or disintegration?

Leadership and the soul

Leadership implies direction. At the most profound level of being (our souls), are we leading toward thriving together or dysfunction, against each other? If we move toward integration, our bodies are doing what we want, and what we want is in alignment with our thoughts, and our thoughts are at peace because of the wellness of our soul. If we are heading in the other direction, then our bodies are directing our wills. Our minds will try to justify unhealthy behaviors but this kills our souls. If left unchecked, our will succumbs to the proverbial tail wagging the dog mode of operations.

When our souls are thrive and center on a source of light, heat, and attraction, we create and sustain liberating cultures. When our souls are failing, we desperately, futilely attempt to control, overprotect, or both. If our souls die, we are apathetic, deadbeat, unmotivated, unable to be motivated—unresponsive.

Where the soul is vibrant and alive, there is freedom. Liberating leaders move toward freedom. From what do we want to be liberated? Outdated rules and limiting beliefs. Myths and temporary fixes passed along to us, likely by those who have not experienced freedom from the oppression of scarcity.

"There's not enough...."

Check out this Bible verse (Habakkuk 2: 4-5) that mentions an enemy puffed up, greedy, and insatiable:
"See, the enemy is puffed up; his desires are not upright—but the righteous person will live by his faithfulness—indeed, wine betrays him;

he is arrogant and never at rest. Because he is as greedy as the grave and like death is never satisfied, he gathers to himself all the nations and takes captive all the peoples."

Notice the last part about gathering all nations and capturing all peoples, very indicative of a familiar societal dynamic. This large-scale enslavement begins with pride and desires that don't align with the universe (time and life). They are not sound, not healthy, and originate from a restless arrogance—unwillingness to believe that there is enough time, provisions, and help at any given time. Yet, there is, if we're open to the possibility that something's missing—i.e., that our beliefs and rules are outdated and limiting, that there are others that are more empowering, relevant, opportunity-seeing, success-finding, and liberating.

In contrast, the righteous are identified by their belief—belief that there is enough, belief that they are enough, that God is enough. A narrative of redemptive sufficiency generates the courage to pursue and be open to options that do not sacrifice relationships or health (spiritual, emotional, physical, mental). I love the words of Lynne Twist:

"Sufficiency is an act of generating, distinguishing, making known to ourselves, the power and presence of our existing resources, and our inner resources. Sufficiency is a context we bring forth from within that reminds us that if we look around us and within ourselves, we will find what we need. There is always enough."[22]

---

[22] Lynne Twist, The Soul of Money, 2003, p.74.

Almost on a daily basis, opportunities for developing liberating leadership pop up. Whether it's with others, ourselves, or within projects that need to get done, there are things that challenge our problem-solving abilities. Some are small, taken care of without much thought or effort. Some require additional learning and strategizing. Some, we've carried with us since the dawn of time, and they chronically plague our relationships. These often have us at a loss as to what to do, or even where to start.

And yet, these challenges contain the potential for substantial, meaningful, sustainable liberation. We tend to avoid them because when they get triggered, all hell breaks loose. We find ourselves desperate, behaving in ways that hurt others and ourselves. They may not be obvious or apparent, but that doesn't mean we haven't generated detrimental, compensatory behaviors. It's possible we simply live with pain, fear, and anxiety, resolved to suck it up and bear it. But the lack of thriving vitality, or at least healthy function, invariably catches up to us, physically, emotionally, relationally, or spiritually. These negative feelings become crises demanding radical change in our models of reality (M.O.R.)[23]. When we're aware of our M.O.R.s, challenges remain incredibly difficult, but at least we have an idea of what's going on. When we don't identify these defaults, it's practically impossible to even understand our challenges; willful blindness is imminent.

This isn't just about relational breakdowns. As a part of a family (or any organization), the consistent relational crises created by

---

[23] Vishen Lakiani, Mindvalley.com, http://blog.mindvalleyacademy.com/tag/models-of-reality

dysfunctional M.O.R.'s impact and influence everyone we're connected to. They becomes the air everyone breathes, the temperature everyone feels, the light that gives sight. When this challenge is not met, tension and stress become normative, resulting in adverse health effects for both parents and children, employers and employees. Growth is stunted, and we don't progress in maturing toward intimacy, generativity, and integrity. Rather, we may very well be headed toward dysfunction, disintegration, and devastation.

But it is in these emotional, relational problems that we can lead ourselves to real freedom and fulfillment. If we center on growth and commit to whatever it takes to create an inner environment for development (e.g. worldview, values, spiritual wisdom), the pains and struggles become breadcrumbs leading us to identify obsolete codes of our operating system, our souls. We remove and replace them. Moreover, in a healthy culture of growth, parents and children become people open to introspection, evaluation, and consistent improvement. They want to be better. They invite it. They create structures for movement. Pixar has several programs in place intentionally fostering collaboration and critique so their films achieve substance to be audience worthy: Dailies, brain trusts, postmortems. Each is a safe space for candor. Everyone feels secure to speak, to share from their hearts about how to improve the project. Working with open feedback, passionate determination for excellence, humility to admit error, need for change, and patience for the process all contribute to "overcoming the hidden forces that get in the way of true inspiration." In the "how" section of this book, there are tools to help you do this.

As you see, it begins with leaders/parents leading themselves intelligently. Negative patterns and cultures grow and perpetuate when we lack M.O.R.s of internal wellness and freedom.

What makes archaic rules and patterns inferior? They produce fear.

Consider Giant Worldwide's Challenge-Support Matrix (see it at https://giantworldwide.com/duct-tape-matrix/). In it, levels of challenge and support we provide determine the roles and cultures we create. Starting with the lower left quadrant, if we don't challenge or support those we live or work with, we are abdicators, cultivating apathy and low expectations. Moving directly to the upper left, with higher levels of support yet lacking challenge, we are protectors fostering entitlement and mistrust. In direct contrast, with high levels of challenge but low support, we end up as dominators who impose fear and manipulation. We want to be in the upper right, with high levels of both. When we challenge with high standards and expectations, alongside substantial support via love and empathy, we are liberators who empower those around us and help them take advantage of opportunities. Fear makes a culture inferior by causing mistrust, entitlement, apathy, low expectations, and manipulation.

For a healthy balance of challenge and support, we need to drive out fear; this is what builds deep trust, unafraid of failure and rejection. Without fear, we communicate openly, honestly, respectfully. Fear can only be effectively and healthily managed by liberating environments, i.e., relationships of true love. The Bible (1 John 4:18) calls it perfect love, meaning love that is mature and complete, without limiting, outdated, inferior M.O.R.s. This is a huge priority for parents, and really anyone who leads and manages groups of people in the creative process.

When we have high demands and expectations within a culture of genuine trust and care, our kids develop the character and ability to excel in their strengths and passions. Nhat Hanh, a Vietnamese monk and peace activist, says, "In true love, you attain freedom." True love does not ineffectively challenge and support; it balances the two, dynamically and wisely applying them according to life stage and individual uniqueness. A healthy soul with empowering beliefs and rules, prioritizes growth, and achieves this connection.

A growth-centered family is led by liberated leaders giving their family members the best. And the best we can give our kids is the leadership of true love*—love that drives out fear, love that attains freedom.* True love is the practice of the liberated. Liberated from what? From the fear based defaults usually adopted and fostered from our youth. Liberated individuals create cultures of empowerment and opportunity; liberty fosters love that drives out fear and builds trust. Most importantly, it frees us to become mature and tap into the untold potential of being growth centered.

Part Two Summary

The universe was created with challenge and support to generate liberating leaders. A growth-centered family is radically, pervasively, uncompromisingly, wholeheartedly, and profoundly embraced by the One Creator. I believe the Creator *is* true love (1 John 4:8), the universal governing principle of the universe who became human—Jesus Christ (John 1:1-4, 14).

Understanding being embraced by something bigger than us reflects a more realistic, relevant, rational perspective. Through a new, powerful, and dynamic set of beliefs and a perspective of being freed from dysfunctional subconscious playback, a new mindset emerges—a growth-centered mindset. And from this, we attain a transformed life and a growth-centered family. A family placing confidence in the primacy and power of applied lifelong learning that results in ongoing development and sustainability—even the incarnation of true love.

I believe this bigger something is God, who is more than enough— more love and grace, more truth and power, more humility and honor than we can imagine. He is true love, and those born of Him (not mildly professed belief, but that birthed in the deepest places of the soul, evidenced by transformed thoughts and actions) live in that love.

"Dear friends, let us love one another, for love comes from God. Everyone who loves has been born of God and knows God. Whoever does not love does not know God, because God is love. This is how

God showed his love among us: He sent his one and only Son into the world that we might live through him. This is love: not that we loved God, but that he loved us and sent his Son as an atoning sacrifice for our sins. Dear friends, since God so loved us, we also ought to love one another. No one has ever seen God; but if we love one another, God lives in us and his love is made complete in us." 1 John 4:7-12

This passage articulates the source of love, the identity and relationship of love's recipients, its corresponding, defining action, our call to action. Having a new sense of belonging to a higher power and acting on this new identity generates a growth mindset. This perspective centers us on doing the things that matter most, that direct us toward a fulfilled life of faith, family, friends, fitness, and even finances. These fulfillments free us from the oppression of fear and insecurity caused by deep, harmful beliefs of scarcity.

When sun-like love is central in our families, we have the primary, essential resource for vision, motivation, doing, and achieving. It helps us create warm, meaningful relationships that can both challenge and support our ongoing development into mature individuals. Parenting with this kind of center is the result of being on the path of transformation, freed from impeding defaults and knee-jerk reactions.

It's amazing how relationships grow and blossom with cultivation of the soul. A thriving soul integrates our hearts and minds to be authentically, positively present. Equally incredible is how relationships foster personal qualities empowering us to succeed: passion, focus, push, ideas, improvement, service, and persistence.

A growth-centered family focuses on creating a culture for healthy, sustainable maturation. This ongoing, positive development allows both parents and kids to take advantage of the many opportunities and resources of each and every moment—good or bad, pain or pleasure, challenge or celebration.

Part Three: Cultivating a Growth Centered Family

Introduction: Prepare to Be a Gardener

Chapter 11: Grow Emotional Energy to Keep Growing

Chapter 12: Grow Healthy Practices and Behaviors

Epilogue: Sustainable Growth

Appendix: Supplemental Tools

Introduction: Prepare to Be a Gardener

Being a gardener means cultivating habits which, if firmly planted in our lives, produce fruit. This means we need to become gardeners. We read this at the beginning of the Bible, and I'd like to take a look at this reference and the immediate context.

"The Lord God took the man and put him in the Garden of Eden to work it and take care of it." Genesis 2:15

The Creator's primary, fundamental purpose for man is cultivation of his environment to generate and sustain life. In this environment, man was given and even directed to eat from all trees except one. This tree was a source of confusion—knowing good and evil.

"And the Lord God commanded the man, 'You are free to eat from any tree in the garden; but you must not eat from the tree of the knowledge of good and evil, for when you eat from it you will certainly die.'" Genesis 2:16, 17

The confusion resulting from eating forbidden fruit, would be a malignant one causing injury, disease, and pain. Further on in the narrative (Genesis 3), we see the fruit of this prohibition was shame and death. Man and woman hid from God, became mortal, and had a son who eventually killed his brother.

Immediately following that instruction and warning comes intention for a helper, a soulmate.

"The Lord God said, 'It is not good for the man to be alone. I will make a helper suitable for him.'" Genesis 2:18

According to this passage, cultivation of the garden is an intimate partnership. This is the ordained design of the family, the primary way for human beings to generate sustainable life—a man and a woman becoming one to create and cultivate an environment in which new life could thrive and care for the world.

What are you cultivating in your home? In your heart? In your relationships? Cultivation takes time, intention, and repetition. Habits, values need to be planted and tended. What they're planted in needs to feed them, just like good soil. Location matters. This may seem obvious, but the thing planted must have the capacity to grow and produce life. What are these things?

Belief, trust, courage, benevolence, are a few. How do we cultivate these intangibles and invisible qualities? We need to grow our knowledge and understanding in the unseen, hidden things—the stuff and forces inside our minds, hearts, and souls. This section delves into these areas, encouraging you to prioritize and commit to growing them. The result is greater insight into helping your family thrive and achieve long-term wellness, fulfillment, and success.

As a gardener, cultivating activities involve caring for your own soul, as well as your relationships with loved ones. Chapter 11 spotlights your interior life, and Chapter 12 and the appendix will present skills and tools for growing clarity and communication taken from sources found in the bibliography. As you develop your practice, it's my hope that you experience more joy, strength, and true love.

Chapter 11: Grow Emotional Energy

to Keep Growing

When things thrive, there's growth. If you're cultivating a garden, that's how you know your plants are healthy—they're getting bigger, maturing, reproducing. As a parent, you want to see your children reach milestones, indicators that they're doing well and developing appropriately. It doesn't stop at adulthood either. Physical growth may reach a limit, but we are not simply physical. We continue to grow mentally, emotionally, relationally, and spiritually without limits.

Growing things need energy. Babies need regular feedings, naps, affection, and stimulation to grow. In the same way, a family centered on growth needs lots of energy to keep things moving forward. This energy comes from different sources—anything fueling, stimulating, encouraging, and inspiring us.

There are things causing us to mismanage or even lose energy. Obviously, if we lack any of the above, we decrease the amount of energy coming to us. But what would cause us to stop doing things that energize us? Here's a list from Guy Winch's *Emotional First Aid*[24]: rejection, loneliness, loss and trauma, guilt, rumination, failure, and low self-esteem. In this chapter, I discuss most of them. These are fear-based, fear-causing, emotional experiences that creep into our souls. They block, drain, and debilitate us from having vitality to keep maturing into our truest, best selves.

The way we handle these emotional challenges can result in greater energy for growth and change or can also diminish our souls.

---

[24] Guy Winch, *Emotional First Aid*, 2013.

Untreated, they disconnect us from the life and love we desire most. If we're going to be deeply connected to our family members, able to walk through thick and thin with them, we need to improve how we deal with those painful struggles. Growth in this area is fundamental to bringing greater joy to our hearts.

Let's turn painful experiences into catalysts to build greater capacity and strength to achieve more of what matters most, starting with rejection.

Overcoming Rejection

Rejection is the most common wound we experience. Dr. Winch likens it to the breaking of our skin. Some cases are minor, like paper cuts. Others can be knife wounds to our gut, causing profuse bleeding externally and internally. It just depends on who it's from and how we're doing at the time of rejection. If these injuries aren't treated, they get infected; profound harm (and even death) can result.

The pain of rejection comes from us being hardwired for connection and belonging. When someone or something makes us feel isolated or unaccepted, it attacks this deep need. The more significant the person or event that rejects us, the closer the trauma is to our vitals. The place in our brains that registers the pain is actually the same as for physical pain.

We do well to become proficient at identifying this emotional hurt and knowing how to treat it. Moreover, we should teach others (especially our children and youth) effective ways to bind up these wounds. Guy Winch calls this emotional hygiene, something we can practice regularly like showering or brushing our teeth. When the injury is profound, we need to seek professional help to heal.

So, here are several ways[25] to treat the pain of rejection and increase your energy for greater growth and change:

Manage Self-criticism

Make a list of negative, self-critical thoughts when you experience rejection of any kind—romantic, family, workplace, social. Develop counterarguments against each self criticism. Take time to internalize your rebuttals so when these reoccur, you can manage them quickly and effectively.

Imagine you're passed over for a promotion at work. Depending on the condition of your soul, you might start creating reasons for the rejection. Somewhere in there are self-deprecating evaluations. The thoughts may not be explicit, but you feel them like arrows.

---

[25] Ibid, pp. 17-35.

Counterarguments help remove the intrusion, cleansing the wound to heal. Honestly describing the bigger picture of your situation offers better understanding of the rejection to determine the real reasons. If one criticism is, "You're too slow. You take too long to get things done." You might counter it with, "I generally take more time to go deeper for issues easily overlooked." Keep in mind that self-criticism is likely not objective; it's a knee-jerk reaction coming from insecurity. If you know that you struggle with self-worth, recruit voices of compassion—yours and others. A key to your argument is your ability to articulate your assets against your desire to beat yourself up.

Clarify Your Worth

Come up with five attributes you highly value about yourself (relevant to the rejection). Choose your top three and write a short essay on each quality's importance to you and how it positively influences your life. Also explain the connection and importance of this characteristic to your self-image. Let's continue with the example above. As a person who is more introspective and exploratory, your highly valuable characteristic could be openness to truth, i.e., wanting to know what's really going on rather than settling for simplistic solutions.

Strengthen Social Connections

Slow down to be more intentional about the people you want in your life. Join support groups and affiliations with a better fit. Keep reminders of family and friends close by, like photos and mementos. Go to a feel good place: your favorite coffee shop, the beach, the lake, and reflect on your closest, most positive relationships. Read meaningful emails and letters. Enjoy photos and videos of loved ones. As ideas come to mind, decide and plan what you will do to foster feelings of acceptance and worth, encouraging yourself to manage negative thoughts aimed to beat you up. Of course, this is extremely significant. Because we need mature, loving people in our lives to move forward, we need to do what's necessary to put ourselves with them.

Overcoming Loneliness

If relationships are what matter most (and they are), then building bigger, stronger, more flexible relationship muscles should be among our top priorities.

What happens when these muscles are weak? We're at risk for loneliness, the first thing God identified as not good. (Genesis 2:18). After each act of creation, God said, "It is good." But after God warned the man of the deadly fruit of the knowledge of good and evil, He made the statement, "It is not good for the man to be alone. I will make a helper suitable for him." The following are symptoms of chronic loneliness[26]:

- Clinical depression
- Suicidal thoughts and behaviors
- Hostility
- Sleep disturbances
- High blood pressure, BMI, cholesterol, and stress hormones
- Decreased immune functions
- Poor decision making, attention, concentration
- As large a risk for shorter life as smoking
- Contagion: spending time with lonely people can increase your loneliness

Loneliness is often-neglected, only increasing its potential to damage. If loneliness is something we're accustomed to, it is more insidious. Because we don't have any point of comparison, the condition continues doing its damage outside our awareness.

There are many causes for loneliness—isolation by physical location of work or home; fear of rejection and emotional pain; or just being too busy. Things get worse when we develop protective/self-hiding attitudes (distrust, suspicion, cynicism, anxiety) and behaviors that atrophy our people-connection muscles.

---

[26]Ibid, p.38.

The cumulative effect is less energy for growth and change. Receptiveness to relationships diminishes. Without the life-giving energy of meaningful, personal connections, we may totally run out of gas for responding to life's challenges and opportunities. Wouldn't you rather head in the opposite direction—knowing and being known? Grow your relational ability and become a lifelong learner who continues to mature in wisdom and grace.

Start with embracing these attitudes for an energy-growing, relationship-muscle-building perspective:

- We aren't at fault for our fears, but our behaviors might be adding to our hurt.
- To overcome our pain, we need to challenge our established perspectives.
- Going against these embedded ways requires emotional risk.
- Risk requires bravery.

Repetition empowers you. Muscle building is about reps, not only during the workout, but also working out over years. Keeping it up and making it a habit transforms your shape, strength, capacities, and abilities. In like manner, to build relational fortitude, regularly engage in these fundamental exercises:

Challenge Negative Perceptions

Remove negatively tinted glasses by fighting pessimism; purposefully visualize yourself successfully overcoming the inclination to withdraw and isolate yourself. Don't be afraid to take small steps, start with showing up and shoot for putting yourself out there for as long as you can. Take a break. Breathe. Do it again. Try to do this at least 3 times, i.e. 3 reps. Each time you do this exercise, you create opportunities for social connection.

Identify Self-defeating Behaviors

Think back to painful or embarrassing relationship events or social settings and identify three behaviors contributing to your lack of connection. *Bravely and mindfully renounce them.* Let them go! If they seem to stick to you, practice. As time progresses, your practice/workout should become more sophisticated by adding other exercises described here. Keep this list handy and review it before connection or social events. Then, engage the battle with negative perceptions using the exercise above. Did I mention this will require courage?

Deepen emotional bonds: Empathize

This requires self-awareness, so we may need to grow that first. Do we tend to avoid conflict and negative emotions? Are we consistently, anxiously trying to please others? Do we swing from extremes of connectivity and isolation? Are we obsessive about control? Do we tend to accept abuse? If we don't know ourselves, it will be very difficult to grasp another's disposition.

Visualize yourself in another's situation in an immersive manner: go to the unnatural space of imagining the other's feelings and capture the other's emotional landscape. Then, returning to your own, review insights thoughtfully. What fears, doubts, and hopes, might they have? What experiences and narratives drive those internal dynamics? And what is their interpretation and perspective on what's going on? This knowledge and understanding of another connects us at a very deep level.

We can be alone and not lonely; we can be lonely though not alone. Being alone can be restorative, but being lonely is toxic. And the less loneliness we have, regardless of age, the more energy we will have for positive growth and development.

Overcoming Loss and Trauma

Going through loss and trauma is devastating. When we lose someone or something of great value or we suffer deep distress, despair, and harmful injury. We experience profound disruptions that rock us to the core. Our lives, identities, beliefs, and relationships are disrupted[27].

According to Dr. Winch, it's just like breaking a bone[28]. The internal structure that supported everything is compromised. Painful and disjunctive, trauma brings all our responsibilities, priorities, and activities to a halt. But with courage, faith, and hard work, there are treasures to be found in the depths.

Treasures of Post-traumatic Growth

Meaningful changes in priorities can happen. Forced to stop the hamster wheel, we have an opportunity to reflect and evaluate what is truly important and what matters most to us and our loved ones. We have the time to think through difficult decisions and make choices that strengthen our resolve, true up our direction, and deepen our sense of purpose.

When we slow down and do less, we're more able to appreciate our relationships. Our view and focus are freed to move from activities to people and our connections with them. This does something invaluable to our souls—we become less anxious, more rested, more at peace. And this is much needed to heal.

---

[27] Ibid, p.75.

[28] Ibid, pp.75-102.

Just like mining requires a lot of work to dig, search, and create accessibility, it's likely that post-traumatic growth treasures require substantial inner life work. But the treasures are greater purpose, fulfillment, peace—are these valuable enough for you to invest your time, effort, and resources?

The area that we'll excavate is our worldview. Why? Traumatic disruptions force new realities on us and challenge our current narratives of who we are and what we think life's about. This causes fear, pain, and grief, and the loss and trauma can define us if we do not heal and recover to the point where we define rather than *be* defined.

Mining activities:

- Immediately after a loss: Talk about it or don't. Depending on how you're wired, not talking may help you heal (by not rehashing the event endlessly in your mind). Or perhaps the opposite is true for you—getting it out may be your way of processing the pain to give you more clarity and peace.
- When you're ready to recover lost aspects of yourself, try this exercise[29]:
  - List 10 positive qualities and characteristics you possessed before the event(s).
  - From the list, identify which qualities you feel are most disconnected/least expressed today.

---

[29] Ibid., p.90-91.

○ For each item, write a brief paragraph about why it's no longer expressed as much as before.

○ For each item, also describe possible people, activities, or outlets you could pursue to express the qualities more than you currently do.

○ Rank items according to which are most doable and emotionally manageable.

○ Set goals for working through the list at a comfortable pace. For example, take on the three easiest ones in the next ninety days. Then, if you're feeling up to it, another three—that'll take you up to the six-month mark. At that point, you can continue with the three-month pace, or you may be ready to envision much larger goals requiring longer amounts of time. From processing your struggles and recovery (the next exercise), you may even be inspired to dream and pursue a top level, life changing goal!

• When you're ready for greater growth, deepen your sense-making[30]. Work at fitting the events into your framework of assumptions and beliefs about the world so they're more understandable, even growing your courage and compassion.

○ Explore why versus repeating how it happened. "Why" triggers a qualitatively different and more productive thought process; answering whys widen our scope of thinking and associations to consider larger

---

[30] Ibid., p.94-95.

existential, spiritual, or philosophical implications and understandings. A bigger picture helps us find meaning and greater internal peace.

○ All this helps break us out of rigid perspectives to consider a larger context and arrive at fresh comprehensions and new perspectives.

- Exercise[31]:

    ○ How would your life be different today if the event hadn't happened?

    ○ In what ways could the outcome of events been worse?

    ○ What factors prevented worse outcomes?

    ○ How grateful are you that worse outcomes didn't happen?

These exercises can be painful, but much like physical therapy after a physical injury, they help strengthen movement and speed up recovery. These processing, restorative activities can help heal and fortify our sense of self and understanding of life. By positioning ourselves to define our losses and traumas, rather than being defined by them, we will discover hidden treasures that fuel our energy for growth and change.

[31] Ibid., p.99.

Overcoming Guilt

Guilt: hero or villain?

Unresolved or excessive guilt will foil your growth plans. Guilt can be a hero and motivate you to make significant, worthwhile change. But don't let it become something that wreaks havoc in your life. Guilt has specific, limited function—to help us right wrongs effectively and equitably. Guilt should not stagnate our growth and development. When we don't manage our guilt, it becomes something that disconnects us from our true selves and our best futures. This is a massive drain on our emotional energy. Losing positive perceptions of ourselves and our destiny dismantles any hope for change and growth.

It's not only the initial wrongdoing and hurt, but rather the ongoing cycles of hurt, guilt, and avoidance/aggression that persist. What may seem innocuous slowly builds to toxic levels poisoning our relationships.

And what about guilt tripping? We may have good intentions to help those we care about change their ways, but all this does is foster resentment, superficiality, perfunctory behavior, and general decline in the relationship. It depletes energy and motivation for true, meaningful change.

How should we deal with guilt so that it doesn't inhibit our forward development? If we appropriately manage guilt, rather than let it manage us, we can use it to strengthen our weaknesses and improve our shortcomings. Without it growing to a villain, we are free to grow in resilience and empathy. Rogue guilt fixates us on unhealthy ways of being and doing. It beats us down and steals our intrinsic dignity. It distorts and even corrupts our perception of others. For example, if I made a devastating mistake which resulted in painful loss, unmanaged guilt could cause me to obsess about never repeating it or attempt perpetual compensation. But life is not about never making mistakes or always trying to make up for something. Moreover, a family cannot be healthy if oppressed by regret and devaluation of self. Life-generating actions are motivated by love and sober valuations. This is why we must develop fortified ways to forgive and be forgiven.

Here are a few suggestions from Dr. Winch[32]:

Render Effective Apologies

We've all been on the giving and receiving ends of apologies, effective ones and failed ones. The following are ingredients that can help substantially. We must acknowledge that we violated expectations, trespassed boundaries, or even caused harm. With a clear statement of regret and admission, we own what we did. Add validating the other person's feelings, then a request for forgiveness. Be ready for that request to be denied, but sensitively pursue it or accept the rejection. It's about the person offended and hurt, not about them forgiving us. With genuine contrition comes humility and patience with the other's

---

[32] Ibid, pp.103-139.

response. Our offer of atonement helps: What can we do or give to tangibly express our regret and sorrow? Again, sensitively respond to their request.

Exercise Self-forgiveness

Along with being forgiven by those we've offended or hurt, we need to forgive ourselves. This increases our ability to enjoy life, and decreases guilt or urges to avoid those we've harmed. We need to decide we've beat ourselves up enough, and we'll make the emotional effort to work through it.

First, take full responsibility and give an honest accounting of the wrongdoing—explicitly acknowledge the action and its impact. Get rid of excuses and extreme condemnation so you can see what was done as objectively as possible. Include an examination of the context; this may involve getting clearer about your life stage and your emotional and mental health at the time. Without greater levels of truth, we remain imprisoned.

Second, intentionally make repairs in the relationship with changes in thinking, habits, behavior, and lifestyle to minimize the likelihood of repeating the offense. This could involve radical change—i.e., the transformation discussed in earlier chapters. But this is sometimes what real forgiveness produces.

We all make mistakes and fail in diverse and numerous ways. It is challenging to have a healthy relationship with guilt, yet essential if we are to continue evolving and maturing into revolutionary agents of positive change. And forgiveness invigorates this relationship.

Overcoming Failure

Do you even know how awesome failure is?

Yes, failures (especially meaningful ones) always hurt, demoralize, and disappoint. And why shouldn't they? Our self-esteem takes a big hit. Our confidence is smitten. Deep fears can be triggered.

Failure is like catching a chest cold[33], and chest colds always feel awful. If untreated, we can end up with pneumonia. Emotionally, that would equate to embedded shame, a chronic sense of helplessness, even clinical depression. The infection arises by ingesting the thoughts of "not enough." I'm not good enough, not smart enough, not important enough; there's not enough time, not enough money. "Not enough" becomes our theme song. If our self-esteem is low, this thought can become a belief that seriously compromises our ability to recover.

---

[33] Ibid, p.173.

The more we believe these negative perceptions about ourselves and our environment (even though they may be totally inaccurate), the more damage we sustain. They mislead us into feeling trapped with very few options—if any—other than giving up. And if we give up, it confirms our "not enough" perception. If not corrected, this can become a mindset. A deep sense of scarcity blinds us from seeing all the support, resources, services, and opportunities that could help us achieve our goals.

So actually, the only thing we don't have enough of is a clear understanding of failure. Failure viewed through a scarcity lens diminishes us. Failure perceived by a mindset of sufficiency empowers. Fearlessly framing failure increases our awareness of our stored capabilities to overcome challenges. If we don't find it within, we find it externally. Failure is actually essential in helping us grow our leadership, strategies, and execution, because it is an indicator that we are engaging a real problem, not a simulation or irrelevant exercise.

This may sound like business talk, but it's just as applicable to the business of raising a family. You cannot raise a healthy and successful family with a mindset and soul shaped by scarcity. Children's first six years are times of absorption from the environment. All the information they receive through their senses shapes their perspective and understanding of life and the world. Even in utero, Mom's blood brings all the emotions, chemicals, and hormones that Mommy experiences. This adds to readiness for growth and development the child needs to become a functioning adult. At birth, what and who the baby sees and hears continue to shape their subconscious. If their parents provide wise, healthy support, they have a foundation of openness to learning and growth, to taking risks, to expressing themselves. But a family environment compromised by instability and insecurity, results in fear and anxiety. It's likely they will struggle with constant needs to be in protection mode, striving for acceptance and adequacy.

A lot of this hinges on how we have dealt with failure. If our responses fostered openness, courage, and love, we are leading our family to grow that kind of culture. If we succumbed to perceptions of scarcity, our home environment may likely be driven by insecurity, anxiety, and worry. And during their early formative years, our kids are simply downloading these signals from their environment, forming the operating system for their future behaviors and attitudes.

Learn to master failure. Consider the following ways to effectively leverage failure to help you elevate your leadership, strategy, and execution:

- See failure as data helping you figure out what you should change in your preparation or execution. When I go fishing and catch nothing, I use the drive home to reflect over what didn't work: the equipment (line size, lures and presentation, rods), the choices I made about where to fish, how long to stay in an area, even my interpretation of the conditions (time of year, water temperature and clarity, wind). I make notes, sometimes mental, sometimes written, about what worked, what didn't, and what to do differently next time. I know failing to catch fish, especially on a recreational level, is not a big deal. Nevertheless for me, it's a hit on my ego.

On a more serious note, when I've made significant, costly mistakes, I definitely felt horrible, humiliated, ridden with guilt. The pain kept me up. The elements that helped me recover were prompt responses of openness to admitting what I'd done, taking responsibility quickly to get ahead of the damage, and noting what I needed to do differently moving forward.

Moreover, it's consistently living from life giving beliefs, values, and perceptions to foster a substantial center of love for self and others. It's creating life-long, soul fortifying disciplines. This intrapersonal foundation gives us the flexibility and mobility to alter the way we think and act in response to failures.

- Use failure to consider new opportunities. Let's say you tried becoming a basketball player and failed. There could be numerous reasons—your size, speed, skills; other players more advanced, an unsupportive coach. You decide to switch sports, maybe football. You discover a passion for it and are successful. Your team goes to the championship and wins! Failure steered you to future success. This actually happened to my son!

- Leverage failure to make you stronger. Diana Nyad is an awesome example of this truth. At age sixty-four, she was the first person to swim from Cuba to Florida. 111 miles, fifty-three hours, no shark cage, and a substantial support team. She achieved at sixty-four what she could not at thirty. She suffered four crushing defeats prior to this. After her first failed attempt, she didn't swim again for thirty years. But incredibly, she found a way to fail three more times and ultimately succeed. It wasn't about being in peak form, but more a story of bold, heroic, even creative determination. Failure can help us identify what to improve. With courage, we can determine the development and resources we need to overcome whatever had stopped us.

• Elevate the significance and value of the journey over success. Recent studies show that making steady progress toward a goal contributes more toward sustained happiness and fulfillment than actually reaching it. In this light, failure loses much of its sting, because it's more about the path and less about the destination.

If you find it difficult to reframe failure, there may be unhealthy, outdated playback/code in your operating system that prevents these suggestions from taking hold. Then the question becomes, will you replace that code? Are you willing to break its ties to you? If not, what makes you want to hold on to it?

Handling failure positively significantly increases energy for ongoing dynamic change and growth. If we mature our perception of failure, we become freer and braver to try things (especially essential when we're stuck). When we're open to new ways, thoughts, and experiences, we are much more likely to take advantage of opportunities for growth and development. Happiness and general wellbeing are additional outcomes.

Key Teaching Elements: Failure, Environment, and Soul

How good are your kids at managing their time? Their emotions? Their pain? Their loneliness? Their boredom? Their freedom? Their contributions to the family (aka chores)? Getting good at managing these life elements are not usually quick lessons to master. They're not going to learn from our verbiage. Yes, we can share how-tos. We should instruct. But if we're not careful, it can easily become blah, blah, blah. We can even model healthy management, but that's still not going to achieve the outcomes we hope for. They'll learn from trial and error. Yep, mistakes and failures. That means two things for us parents:

1. We need to give them opportunities to try, fail, learn, try again, and repeat. Of course, we're talking affordable mistakes, not falling so hard that there's irreparable damage. Very subjective, I know. Read on.
2. We also need to create a learning environment in our home, i.e. empowering relationships with empathy before consequences. Get sad instead of mad, but remain firm. Be real about our own weaknesses, struggles, and failures, but also show authentic learning and change to be and do differently. Be teachable, most importantly

with regards to inner life dynamics—caring for the soul. Basically, synthesize everything I've shared.

A healthy soul helps us do all this and distinguish affordable mistakes from unaffordable ones. When we are not controlled by busyness, restlessness, insecurities, anxieties, and neglect of self (results of not caring for our souls), we will be able to see opportunities and create supports needed for our children to get the most learning from the challenges of mistakes and failures. With the proper environment and plenty of practice, our children develop capacity, competence, and confidence in their own learning, resilience, and decision making. The result is increasing responsible independence.

So, stop avoiding failure. In your pursuit for perfection, courageously put yourself in positions to fail. Nowhere does it say that perfectionists can't be vulnerable. Doing so will actually elevate the outcomes of your meticulous perfectionism! What will happen to the world when all the gifts, energy, and strengths of perfectionists get applied to problems that require failure—and possibly lots of it—to figure out. Encourage coworkers, students, and family members to not fear failure, but to be free to learn from their mistakes. And be sure to consistently work on your own healthy openness to failure and learning from it.

Overcoming Low Self-Esteem

What benefits do we get from a strong, stable sense of self-worth?

Well, it's like a healthy immune system[34]. We're less vulnerable to attacks from rejection and failure. We bounce back quicker from setbacks. We're better at learning from mistakes. We're less chronically stressed because we're able to set healthy boundaries to balance our lives. We have energy to healthily develop ourselves through each life stage.

On the other hand, what happens to us if our self-esteem is low? Self-blame. We take things too personally, making negative feedback more stressful. This results in less self-control, increasing the weight of mistakes and failures, which then leads to more self-blame—a vicious cycle. We experience more pain from rejections and failures. This can cause us to lose sense of who we really are and become something we're not. We're less persistent after failures and overgeneralize their meaning. Then, we don't learn what we need. We're more vulnerable to anxiety and depression. We tend to have higher retention of cortisol in our blood, bringing a host of physical ailments.

What happens if we do nothing about it? We're less likely to recover from loss and trauma. We're less adaptive. We isolate ourselves to minimize risks of rejection and pain. We increase self-protection, decreasing openness to emotional nutrients, help, and support. With

---

[34] Ibid, p. 213.

cortisol accumulation come high blood pressure, poor immune systems, suppressed thyroid glands, reduced muscle and bone density, and even poor cognitive performance.

If unaddressed, feeling unworthy becomes a part of our identity. We resist positive affirmation and encouragement. We reject everything and everyone that does not align with our negative self-perceptions—this is very problematic in personal relationships.

So how do we increase our sense of self-worth? Here are some starters:

- Embrace the fact that we need to strengthen our emotional immune systems (self-esteem), not beat them down.
- Purge emotionally abusive voices in our heads; adopt kinder/ more supportive ones.
- Get rid of the belief that more self-compassion causes slacking off and decrease performance (resulting in lower self-esteem).
- Exercise to fortify low self-esteem: Identify and affirm strengths
    - Get two pieces of paper.
    - On first sheet, list ten of your attributes and achievements that are most meaningful to you.
    - While brainstorming, write any negative/ sarcastic thoughts on second sheet.
    - Pick the most important item from the first sheet and write a brief essay on why it holds such value and what you hope it will do for you in the future.

- Once your essay is completed, crumple the second sheet and throw it into the garbage.
- On subsequent days, pick another item and write about it in like manner.

For additional exercises, go back to the suggested treatments for rejection, loneliness, guilt, and failure. Create a workout regimen to grow your courage, which will increase the clarity and confidence of your self-worth.

We aren't shooting for high self-esteem, which resembles narcissism. It's more about a healthy sense of self-worth giving us both confidence and humility with openness to emotional pain, but also the ability to manage it effectively. Strong and stable self-esteem energizes us to be courageous, compassionate, and candid. Its primary purpose is to help us connect meaningfully and appropriately to those who matter most to us.

Closing Thoughts

To grow, we need energy. Just plain ole science. No energy, no growth. How we deal with emotional challenges can either increase or deplete our energy. They can stop us from progressing in our personal growth as adults—much more for children who may not have the awareness, abilities, capacities, or resources to deal with them.

Effectively overcoming these challenges is what helps us meet our deficient needs (Maslow's hierarchy), especially for love, belonging, and esteem. It's these middle levels where many people get stuck, especially in societies and cultures that neglect the inner life, prioritizing and focusing on performance, achievements, and external success.

Inner-life work is essential to develop and strengthen each family member's worldview, foster emotional health, overcome hurts, resolve conflicts, and progress toward greater maturity. It's a primary way for growth-centered families to have the energy to progress through the various stages of psychosocial development (Erikson). Much of this work is forming, developing, and transforming beliefs that free us to love others and ourselves in healthier, wholehearted ways. Growing one's faith and perceptions is one of the most radical determinants of how we love. We need beliefs and perspectives that generate courage, fortitude, forgiveness, joy, and compassion. Without these powerful, positive emotions, our actions will not consistently express the love our families need and want. When our love falls short and relationships suffer, you can trace it to fear-based beliefs. But when we do the arduous work of examining and changing our faith and how we express it, we embark on the journey of transformation. With the levels of family dysfunction in the world, it's not hard to see that we have a faith crisis that shows up in how we love throughout our lifespan.

This is fundamentally important for young people as they go from building trust to discovering identity. What they believe about life, themselves, others, and God has a huge impact on their emotional hygiene and profoundly affect their emotional energy for ongoing growth into adults.

Faith and its formation is critical for parents who create and cultivate the home environment—i.e., the preconditions for growth of the ones under their care. That means the milestones (of intimacy, generativity, and integrity), the path, and the energy for adult growth must be given first –priority—above and beyond the daily responsibilities, distractions, and worries. Doing so will aid filtering of what is "good" versus what is best for our families. I put good in quotes because most if not all parents are doing what they believe to be good, i.e. being overly responsible for their children, not letting them struggle or fail. But this is far from best as it derails children from becoming responsible for themselves. When we prioritize our own emotional wellness rather than being anxiously driven to help/control our children, parenting also becomes less stressful and more joyful.

With high levels of emotional health and hygiene, all family members continue on the path to become their very best, living up to their highest potentials—physically, morally, spiritually, professionally. Perpetual energy to grow is what we all need to hear our calling and be visionary leaders in our families, our communities, and our work.

We need a center that grows emotional energy rather than drain it. What centers our lives (Chapter 8) is a potent source of either peace or chaos. If the center is a massive source of light and warmth, our lives stabilize in their orbits. But if the center is unsubstantial and does not create a consistent place of visibility and comfort of inner life dynamics, we are at the mercy of our fight or flight responses, with nothing to keep us on the path to greatest fulfillment and meaningful success for ourselves and our loved ones.

Chapter 12: Grow Healthy Practices

& Behaviors

Overview

Much of our lives is spent doing the same things again and again, week after week, month after month, and so on. For myself, I want my life to become a set of actions that continually grow me and those I love and serve to be our best. I started Part Three of this book with the metaphor of gardening.

When it comes to supporting the growth of our families in what matters most—our souls, relationships, and leadership—we need regular activities to expand, deepen, and fortify our interior lives and our connections with each other's hearts. The practices in this section include skills and tools to develop your emotional hygiene, parenting, and spiritual growth.

The way we care for ourselves emotionally has profound, long-term impact on how we sustain ourselves. Successfully raising kids takes certain capacities and skills which can and should be learned and applied. Spirituality—that is, living according to unseen, intangible principles and forces that connect us with God, others, and ourselves—empowers us with wisdom, motivation, liberty, courage, and resolve.

Teaching, Training, Discipline

When inner life and relational needs are regularly met, we can confidently teach, train, and discipline. We're ready to implement limits with love and empathy. Raising kids effectively is not a monolithic activity. It has to be healthy, which means it has to be balanced with challenges and support. And the shaping and influencing of our children does not consist of quick fixes and overnight changes. Effective training and development is a matter of consistent implementations of limits, consequences, and conversations. To do this well, we need the capacity for constancy and dedication, as well as skills to implement disciplinary measures.

If we want our kids to achieve autonomy, initiative, and industry, they need to learn age-appropriate limits and disciplines that strengthen them physically, mentally, emotionally, relationally, and spiritually. Yes, conversations are needed and helpful, but we mustn't neglect the role of consequences. Our conversations will become meaningless if we do not utilize negative outcomes to teach our kids that we mean what we say and we say what we mean. They need to fail and experience real results in order to figure out what they will do differently the next time. We should anticipate failures and their consequences as learning opportunities; not to rub our children's noses in them or say, "I told you so." But to allow the outcomes to teach real limits. We don't want to cause a development deficit by keeping affordable mistakes from teaching our kids. We want to be brave and compassionate facilitators of this real-life learning. In addition to having the patience and fortitude to empathetically enforce consequences, the challenge for us here is to discern which mistakes are affordable and which ones are not.

To be able to challenge and support them in this development, we will need to establish the foundations discussed in the first two parts of this book. It'll be nearly impossible for us to teach, train, and discipline if we ourselves haven't been trained and disciplined. If we were fortunate enough to have parents or mentors who did this, we're off to a great start. If not, we have the arduous task of figuring things out as adults. The tools at the end of this section will be helpful with this.

If we're open to learning about and exploring our interior lives, I'm confident great things will happen. Find your courage. Find its source. Then plant yourself there and experience a growth-centered life.

Setting Boundaries[35]

Why set boundaries? They help us live successfully, enabling us to navigate and relate to things and people effectively. They foster trust. They define us and help others know and understand us. Without them, relationships suffer and trust dissolves. Without authentic connections bolstered by healthy limits and boundaries, life gets reduced to manipulation, apathy, mistrust, and a train of negative perceptions and emotions.

---

[35] The Parenting Children's Course (Alpha International, 2011), pp.35-40

Boundaries set by unconditional love are essential to effective and appropriate discipline. This means they must be a logical, reasonable synthesis of love and limits. A child naturally wants and needs to know where the limits/boundaries/rules are and who is going to enforce them. This is a profound, fundamental requirement to build the trust and security children use to support their exploration into their stages of autonomy and initiative. Healthy, effective boundaries both protect and encourage them to define, discover, and develop self-control, respect for authority, and a sense of security. This helps them develop effective filters and ideologies—worldviews—that serve and mature them into healthy, loving individuals.

Boundaries are absolutely necessary to becoming highly moral, creative problem solvers who not only positively impact the world, but also help others do the same. Healthy limits both protect and empower us by teaching us to find better and better ways to fulfill all of our needs. When we can recognize the limits of what we're doing and what they do to us, we can make wise choices that prevent us from blind conformity. A great example is sleep. Just learning to respect the limits of our bodies and minds by giving them adequate rest keep them working at optimum levels. Add to this the habits of healthy diets and exercise routines, and we're on our way to consistent improvement and renewal.

Now add the defining boundaries and principles of self-care and soul keeping, and you increase your mastery and stewardship of your entire being. This empowers you to truly set yourself apart from societal dysfunctions and large-scale epidemics of collusion, corruption, and conformity. You will instead be a transformative agent in the big picture of human history.

"Transformation is the context in which history makes sense.... When we are being transformed, we are coming to the place where history makes sense as we are part of the fulfillment of history - our own as well as that of the world.... Our current roles involve hospicing the dead and dying ways rather than being midwives to the birthing of the new."
—Lynne Twist[36]

Bringing this back to parenting, the dynamic, age-appropriate boundaries we set should teach, train, and discipline our children to develop into people who achieve more of what matters most, with solutions to move us all forward. We don't need cowardice, conformity, corruption, collusion, or all the chaos that oppresses and exploits life. Through healthy teaching, training, and disciplining, let's foster courage, love, and wisdom that exponentially improves life for all people across all sectors and industries.

What is your parenting style? Are you authoritative? Authoritarian? Permissive? Uninvolved? Here are some potential indicators to help you determine your inclination[37]:

---

[36] Lynne Twist, *The Soul of Money*, 2003.

[37] https://www.parentingforbrain.com/4-baumrind-parenting-styles/

Children of Uninvolved Parents:

- Are more impulsive.
- Cannot self-regulate emotion.
- Encounter more delinquency and addictions problems.
- May struggle intensely with mental illness.

Children of Permissive Parents:

- Cannot follow rules.
- Have worse self-control.
- Possess egocentric tendencies.
- Encounter more problems in relationships and social interactions.

Children of Authoritarian Parents

- Tend to have an unhappy disposition.
- Are less independent.
- Appear insecure.
- Possess lower self-esteem.
- Exhibit more behavioral problems.
- Perform worse academically.
- Have poorer social skills.
- Are more prone to mental issues.

Children of Authoritative Parents

- Appear happy and content.
- Are more independent.
- Achieve higher academic success.
- Develop good self-esteem.

- Interact with peers using competent social skills.
- Have better mental health—less depression, anxiety, suicide attempts, delinquency, alcohol and drug use.
- Exhibit less violent tendencies.

We want to create and enforce limits, without extremes of harshness or permissiveness, balanced. We should aim for being dynamically authoritative, not static, because our loved ones are always evolving. To be relevant and effective where they are, our presence also needs to evolve to help them grow ways to meet their own needs and respond to boundaries and limits.

We want to teach them to question and challenge limits. We want to teach wise and healthy choices and the corresponding consequences occurring in the real world, not just Mom and Dad's world. Instruct and explain behaviors and their outcomes regarding how we manage and prioritize our time, money, relationships, self-care, and soul keeping.

Let results and consequences teach, whether they occur according to natural laws or they are created by us (i.e. taking something away or giving a time out). Give them freedom to choose and make (affordable) mistakes. This educates them in responsibility for their own actions. Allow or apply negative consequences with empathy, not anger and frustration. The ultimate purpose—and we mustn't overlook this—is for our kids to learn to think for themselves, for their evaluations and reflections to deepen and become more objective as time goes on. The main thing is the learning and application.

When a conflict or contention occurs, do not react negatively; think about what you want to do, with the exception of scolding, nagging and/or lecturing. Very rarely do we need to do something immediately. Exceptions, of course, are situations where physical injury or death is imminent. Otherwise, take time to get clear about the context, the bigger picture. Start with some current whys. Use the following acronym HALT[38] to pause and think about why you and your loved ones are having tension.

- H - hunger?
- A - anxious?
- L - lonely?
- T - tired?

That is the immediate context. If you recognize one or more of those factors in either or both of you, address that first. Let's get some yummy food. Or provide some comforting words and appropriate touch. Or let's just get some sleep or rest.

In addition to HALT, let's also look at a bigger picture in setting appropriate boundaries, using Erikson's psychosocial stages. What's the struggle, or what we want to develop? Say we are telling our toddler that it's time to put away toys and wash up for bed. She resists. "No. I don't want to." What do you do?

A. Put your foot down.

---

[38] The Parenting Children's Course (Alpha International, 2011), p.52.

B. Permit them to keep playing.

C. Provide a time limit.

All three have their place, depending on the context. Let's start with Maslow. Are their physiological, safety, and love needs met? If they are, let's consider their psychosocial stage. As toddlers experience the world, they learn that actions get results. They're developing likes and dislikes, working towards independence. This is the "me do it" stage. A two-year-old child may want to choose her clothes and dress herself. The outfit may not be the best choice for the situation at hand, but being able to decide affects her sense of independence. If parents consistently choose for her, she may begin to doubt her abilities, develop low self-esteem, and feelings of shame.[39] With this element to consider, providing a time limit both honors her choice (support autonomy) and gets her to bed at an appropriate time (immediate practical need).

Now, what happens if time is up and she still says no? That's where the proof is in the pudding. Do you mean what you say and say what you mean? More importantly, what kind of limit enforcer are you? Will you enforce with empathy or exasperation? Now, let's expand the context (adding to HALT, hierarchy of needs, and psychosocial development stage) to include your own inner landscape. This involves at least a couple factors.

1. What is your general emotional status; i.e., your overall mood, the climate generated by your presence?

---

[39] https://www.boundless.com/psychology/textbooks/boundless-psychology-textbook/human-development-14/theories-of-human-development-70/erikson-s-stages-of-psychosocial-development-269-12804/

2. What is your understanding and ideology about your child's behavior and development?

Are you clear about their needs for limits and encouragement? Do you have a healthy perception of their youthful insecurity and evolving personality?

These two elements create the story you tell yourself, which determines your feelings and behavior in moments of contention. Consistency is what makes or breaks our tactics. Training requires repetition. Some kids need more reps than others. Toddlers usually take 700 falls to figure out how to walk. How many times will yours need to learn to listen and follow your directions? How many bad choices does a child need in order to learn how to make good ones? Whatever the number may be, we need to have the patience and fortitude to both challenge and support them in this highly significant development.

Providing healthy, effective limits will help with the learning, discernment, and leadership necessary to move forward. Boundaries keep kids on track to figuring things out without the extra, painful baggage of shame, anger, repression, guilt, and insecurity from a lack of a loving, authoritative, secure individual.

As we set limits, we should be growing the quality of our thoughts and actions to adjust to changing circumstances. Recognize natural childishness, the difference between immaturity and disobedience. Adjust expectations and responses according to levels of development. Consistently implement limits, rules, and boundaries, but do so with healthy levels of humor to lighten the atmosphere. Laugh together with your spouse and other parents as you work on this incredibly important aspect of parenting. Team up to create training opportunities for your kids to learn from the limits you implement.

Boundaries and Decisions

Boundaries define shape. Shape determines function. Function creates value and generates identity. Think of a stream of water. Its boundaries limit where and how it moves. People have built dams to reshape streams into larger bodies of water for energy, conservation, and recreation. These functions have increased the value of the stream for humans, and we come to identify them as great resources that provide, sustain, and promote life.

In like manner, the boundaries we set can help our kids become great decision makers who contribute value to society, from high-quality service and work to raising another generation of great decision makers. What kinds of boundaries move things in this direction?

Here's a list of fundamentals:

1. Be fair and clear

This is foundational for development in making good choices. We help them define what is fair and what's not and how to discern it. It's essential that parameters are consistent but not statically simple.

This means we have to be clear. Are they old enough to understand our instructions? Do they need to understand immediately, or can we teach it gradually? They don't have to like our limits, but as they get older and their thinking gets more developed, will the limit make sense? It's absolutely essential that we aren't simply setting limits blindly according to outdated rules and limiting beliefs. This is a big reason for growing our interior lives—so we get clearer about our own values, beliefs, and behaviors. If these elements aren't clear, we will set boundaries that cause our kids to become confused and stumble. You may want to go back to Chapter 8 to refresh this connection to transformation.

2. Use your voice and "no" effectively

Communication is huge. For the most part, our tone should be casual and comfortable. We want to make ourselves easy to talk to and easy to listen to. Consistent extremes compromise conversations and kill desire to be with each other. Our voices should cultivate love and belonging, esteem and friendship.

There are times to use a serious tone to teach what "no" means. This doesn't require being mean or sounding angry, though it may be perceived that way. It is about not making it sound like a joke or something you don't mean. It is being firm and expressing the gravity of the limit with confidence and conviction.

More important is what to do if and when the limit is crossed. At this point, we actually want to limit speaking and let actions speak. When our kids experience negative outcomes without negative emotions from us, it is a powerful moment that communicates not only boundaries, but the kind of person enforcing the rules. This impacts and influences the development of our children's perceptions. It is a significant part of their growth toward becoming free from outdated and limiting rules and beliefs. Then, they can discover their uniqueness and power to live wisely and purposefully.

Aim not to shout unless you're alerting them to danger. Actions get results. Shouting, nagging, lecturing, and threatening are only effective in stopping our kids from learning, making positive changes on their own, and listening for and to their own voice, even their soul.

To reiterate, consequences make our boundaries effective. But these are not about punishment; they aren't intended to make sure our kids "learn their lessons." They should serve the purpose of helping our kids think, clearly, deeply, and authentically so they can figure out and decide what they want to do. The most important developmental, empowering choice is not simply what they want, but deciding what *to* want. Our explanations and verbal acumen can never teach this. If we try, it quickly becomes a form of manipulation as we try to persuade them to doing want what we want. This also means our consequences should not shame or guilt our kids into choosing to do what we want. If this makes sense, great. If not, you may need to get clear about what you really want. Perhaps you haven't been given the time and opportunities for that. Educating our wills is a lifelong endeavor; it's extremely important and powerful, but easily overlooked due to the plethora of distractions of busyness.

3. Be proactive and intentional

Structure regular family meetings to talk about goals, challenges, and concerns. Encourage sharing with unloaded questions and nonjudgmental answers. Discuss concerns and rules to clear up expectations and consequences. Share about your own goals and struggles, and invite each family member to support you with encouragement and accountability. This can be a great time to model and foster vulnerability and real courage that can be continued one on one with each other at other times.

Structuring in these times gives a platform for every member of the family to express and talk about whatever is on their minds and hearts. It also helps identify, more explicitly, the direction and progress of each member. As you facilitate this ongoing discipline, you can gain a greater awareness of what your family is about—not only from what each member shares, but how each member engages or does not.

This should not be a stress-producing time; there shouldn't be any pressure to perform, impress, or conform. To make this time valuable and productive, you'll need to be working on the general climate of relationships. If the air is good, family meetings will have a much greater chance of being useful and sustainable. If relationships aren't healthy, then that needs to be prioritized. The family meeting can be a time to address this, but only if parents (at least one) are ready to be vulnerable and lead the needed change to improve connections.

4. Give choices

Making choices, good and bad, is a very important part in growing wisdom for success and development. In order to make good decisions consistently, bad decisions are needed to help the good ones stand out. And as time goes on, the weight of the decisions should increase; our children need them in order to practice life without us. This also gives them the confidence of deep, healthy esteem. Gradually increase the importance of choices given as they age. Here are some examples of simple choices:

- Which two toys do you want to take?
- Do you want to go to the beach or the park?
- Do you want to have a snack first or after you finish your homework?

As your kids become adolescents, give them choices concerning their growing responsibilities, such as contributions at home, work at school, and time for self and family.

- When are you going to pick up and switch the laundry?
- What will you do about your grades in math?
- When do you want to spend time with us?
- How do you want to better manage your time?

Some of you may be thinking that giving your children these choices will create more problems than peace. You're absolutely right, they will. And that's exactly what needs to happen. It's the prevention of problems and the drive to do so that snowballs into cultures of ineffective parenting strategies. The messiness sets the stage for the re-creation and perpetuation of a growth-centered culture.

Giving choices helps our kids learn from mistakes and successes. But more importantly, choices shape our culture. Healthily managing bad decisions with empathy and consequences does a ton to empower our teaching, training, and disciplining of our precious ones. It also increases our children's ownership of their choices and gives them greater self-esteem, since we express belief in them to figure things out. This communicates unconditional love, the ultimate value in the culture we want for our homes.

5. Stay calm and in control

Avoid getting sucked into shouting matches. Our negative emotional responses can give our kids a sense of power over us. Push Mom's buttons. Pull Dad's triggers. Don't be manipulated by your children's shouting, whining, or tantrums. To stay in control and keep your composure and sanity, simply say, "No problem," and walk away for the time being. Then, work on appropriate, easy-to-execute responses and consequences. Ask your spouse, friends, or family members for suggestions.

Also you'll want to prepare for any backtalk and arguing. Because when the moment comes to deliver the consequence, there's a high likelihood for resistance. So be ready with an empathetic one-liner, responding calmly by reminding why it's happening. If your child proceeds to shout, whine, or throw a tantrum, use your one-liner and implement the consequence. Do not explain. Do not lecture. Do not engage with reason. Do not get sarcastic. Rather, say nothing that directly engages their complaints. There can be time for dialogue but in the heat of the moment is not the time.

Here are some suggestions, but feel free to come up with your own:

- "I know."
- "I understand but this is still going to happen."
- "We can talk afterwards."
- Give a sympathetic groan.
- Use a counting system[40]: If your child argues or whines, say, "That's one." If your child continues, "That's two." Another resistant response, "That's three. Take five (minutes of time out)." (Dr. Phelan recommends the number should equate to one minute per year of life.)

If they promise to change and do better next time, reassure they'll get the opportunity but bravely stand behind the consequence and let it happen. There's been times where I followed through but regretted it as it was too much for the infraction. In those moments, I went to my child, apologized, explaining my faulty thinking, and changed things mid-stream. If I came to the realization afterwards, I apologized and shared my regret and why. I also made the adjustments in my disciplining for future situations.

6. Follow through with consequences

---

[40] Dr. Phelan and Costanzo, *1-2-3 Magic: Effective Discipline for Children 2-12, 6th ed. 2016.*

Most of the time, consequences should be implemented immediately upon an infraction. Don't use idle threats; only give warnings that you will go through with. Start with small consequences with short durations and give your kids a chance to try again. This diffuses tension, lightens the load, and gives everyone space to breathe and think. If your child repeats poor decision making, gradually increase the severity. In addition, keep a dialogue going for you and your child to be clear about what's going on and why—that the consequence is not going to change behavior. The consequence is not a punishment, but rather a reminder to think about decisions and behaviors and to make changes for the better.

A consequence usually falls into several categories: loss of something (toy, time for desired activity, a privilege) or a natural outcome of their action/inaction (being cold because they didn't want to bring a jacket; being hungry because they refused to eat what was served).

Some of you might have problems with this. But realize that kids do not learn from telling, threatening, reminding, nagging, lecturing, etc. Consequences teach; but they will only teach what we want taught in the absence of strong negative parental emotions like fear-inducing anger and frustration. When we empathetically but firmly execute consequences or allow poor decisions to have their natural outcomes, we stay in control and create space for learning. Explicit learning may not happen immediately. If it does, it's likely superficial. But the patience of a parent's self-control and the consistency of a child's opportunity to learn from choices and consequences go a long way toward cultivating real trust to foster growth and development.

7. Work together

When both parents are involved, agree on a strategy, consistent, and ready to support each other, setting boundaries will be easier and more effective. And if you're a single parent, invite trusted adults to be a part of your team. Healthy collaboration multiplies our smarts and divides our burdens. Share your vision of being growth centered with them and work together to create a better world for you, them, and your kids.

As everyone develops in the midst of a growth-centered culture, boundaries contribute to the health and joy of everyone in the home. But more important than the boundaries is a liberating spirit of working together through the struggles and pains of becoming great decision makers. This investment prepares you to invite your children to discuss more serious choices and how to entrust them to make wise decisions.

Encourage Problem Solving

Helping our kids become great problem solvers is a gift that keeps on giving. We have to remember that it's not what we do for our kids that will make them successful, but rather what we help them do for themselves. If we develop this skill, we experience awesome benefits as well. We'll take better care of ourselves by not getting pulled into every problem. Our relationship with our kids will be healthier because we're building trust with each other; we show we believe in our children's abilities and they trust we are not trying to control them. Ultimately, our kids will grow autonomy by being less dependent on us for things they can take care of.

Again, it begins with empathy; we want to consistently cultivate the learning environment. This is such an important point to drive home. Our own emotional health is absolutely essential if learning and growth are priorities for our family.

You hear, "He's messing with my stuff...she keeps bothering me...I can't do this...I can't find my...." A problem has appeared.

Don't go for the quick fix by giving advice. Instead, coach them with this simple process:

Start by simply asking, "What's wrong?" or "What happened?" This is only to get them to think about it, not necessarily for your understanding and assessment. Then ask them what they want to do. If they don't know and want help, offer some suggestions. Remember, they don't have to be good ones; we actually want them to come up with their own. After offering some ideas, ask, "Will those work for you?" Freely allow them to accept or reject them. Show no partiality so you don't influence their decision. Our primary objective here is to help our kids get better at problem solving and this doesn't depend on advice from us. It depends on our ability to listen, hand the problem back, and create the opportunity for them to explore solutions.

Remember, we do not want to actually help them solve the problem. We want them to do it. But we can take advantage of the opportunities that our children's problems create. Our intentionality can lessen our stress and produce more responsible kids.

The Long Term Goal

When we consider our long term aim, we want to encourage responsibility and train for healthy independence[41]. We don't own our children. They need to own their lives when they become adults. It's our job to prepare them. We need to be intentional about moving control from us to them. Letting go can be hard. Thank goodness it's a gradual, eighteen-year process. We have this period of time to train them and ourselves for healthy independence. The way this is done influences both them and us. How we manage ourselves and our children will have substantial effects on how they manage themselves. If we want them to lead themselves and wisely steward their time and resources, we need to be intentional about ways to truly help them develop values that show up in their actions.

When they do become adults, what kind of moral framework do you want them to have? What information and values do you want to

---

[41] The Parenting Children's Course (Alpha International, 2011), pp.61-66.

pass on to them? Whatever they may be, realize and embrace the fact that consequences (regardless if they're positive, negative, or neutral) are the most effective teachers. They are the elements that most foster and influence the development of responsible choices. Our children need to connect outcomes with their own decisions, not what we tell them. When we make it about us, they won't own and develop their ability to judge and discern what they want or what is best for them.

Moral Framework/Unifying Principles
Choices
Experiences/Consequences
Choices

What do you want for your children in that top circle?

What choices will help them develop it?

What experiences and consequences will support those significant decisions?

What choices do they need to practice on a regular basis?

Sure, our advice and input helps. But don't mistake it for your educational bread and butter; it should only be seasoning. Allow them to make their own decisions and learn from their mistakes. We just want to make sure we create a culture conducive to learning and that empowers trial applications and ongoing modifications. That is, it's safe to mess up, to make wrong decisions. Yeah, the consequences might make life harder and temporarily more chaotic, but with emotional, spiritual, and relational health, we can figure things out, resolve issues, and come out stronger and wiser. More importantly, trust is deepened, conflict is not scary, and courage grows. This is the meat and potatoes of developing long-term goals of responsibility and capabilities for adulthood.

What prevents our kids from learning true independence? Unhealthy control. This can be caused by wanting to look good, projecting "what's best for you," fear of failure, stress, or perfectionism —all fear-driven attitudes. Here are three common symptoms.

1. Micro-managing

Can anyone say, 'helicoptering'? This is over-protection and always rescuing our kids from consequences of poor choices, whether it's not listening and following instructions to forgetting to take care of a responsibility.

Of course, I need to point out here affordable mistakes versus ones that can cause long term disabilities and irreparable harm. Too often, parents don't make intelligent, rational distinctions - thinking everything that causes emotional distress isn't affordable. This could be an indicator of a parent's unmet needs for security, love and belonging, and maybe even esteem. Or perhaps it's even more basic; they just need to improve the meeting of their physiological needs, ie. sleep, diet, excretion, etc.

If we don't stop 'helicoptering', our kids may be at risk for lacking responsibility, decreasing learning about life and poor decision making skills.

2. Being over-competitive

When we are driven about our kids' success, we may be putting undue pressure on them. And when we do this, what's the underlying message? Winning equates to success and happiness? Winning trumps relationships? You are more important than everyone else? Sacrifice everything for the win - time, resources, energy, relationships, even character.

Nothing wrong with competition as long as it is framed and managed by healthy values. But if it comes from a place of unmet needs (Maslow's hierarchy) and gets in the way of positive psychosocial development, we ought to back off and reevaluate what our kids need to become responsible in the best possible ways.

3. Over-scheduling

Stanford University's education department's mantra is "Challenge Success." They've done research and development to help parents and schools find alternate modes and methods for success. Over the last several decades, they've not only recognized the harm in over-scheduling, they've identified and promoted the need for PDF—play, down, and family time. They've found this is key, not only to academic success but real, sustainable success and fulfillment in life, both at work and home.

Something to get clear about—what's driving it all? Is it a fear of missing out or being left behind in the "human race"? (It''s not really a race.) Is it coming from a scarcity mindset? It's extremely difficult to cultivate a growth environment without meeting essential needs for empowering relationships, and soulful reflection and nurture, plus some good ole "R & R." Recall Chapter 8: "Soulful," meaning our souls need rest so we can slow down and reflect. This is needed to make sense of things, especially the more complex stuff that involves negative experiences and emotions—the stuff we tell ourselves we don't have time for. All this does is perpetuate attitudes and behaviors that keep us stuck in unhealthy ways of relating to our loved ones. If our kids get caught up in this dysfunction, their healthy independence may be challenged and even compromised, but it will be stinted for sure.

When it comes to our schedules, less is often more. A slower pace creates more time and space for meaning—making, less stress hormones in our blood. This creates, over time, a trajectory toward healthy maturation; and this progress leads to healthy independence. If we're not used to this, it will be initially uncomfortable, but it will be worth it to make sense of the deeper complex issues we may be avoiding or unaware of. Slow down to go farther, stronger, longer. This is the only way to discover and achieve long-term goals—goals that benefit everyone. It's the road to win win solutions not apparent when we're overbooked, overstressed, and overcome by the beast of productivity.

Helping Our Kids Make Good Choices

In our current society, there are three big areas in which our children need to make important choices—sex, the internet/video games, and drugs/alcohol. Actually, all three can be traced to how we find comfort from stress and pain. How we deal is core to who we are and the story we write. Our identity is defined by how we manage desires and pain. We want to bring these topics into the light for our kids to see clearly what they're about, but we will also want to have these conversations in a warm environment, without fear and judgment. High levels of love help us learn best, and this is true for young ones. When our families are growth-centered, cultivating what matters most, everyone is more aware of what good choices are and how to make them.

Sex

With sex, we need to drip-feed information from a young age. Be proactive, so no one beats you to educating your kids about this deep, intimate, profound area of life. Answer their questions honestly and accurately; use opportunities for conversations, such as magazine articles, internet posts, TV shows, or movies. Talking and teaching about sex is less awkward when you both care deeply about the soul and prioritize healthy relationships. If these essentials aren't in place, talking about sex comes across as something disconnected from reality, walled off as weird or perverse.

Talk about "right and wrong touch". More importantly, model what is authentic, affectionate, and appropriate. This is a one-two punch protecting our children with discern danger and desire safe relational touch.

As children approach puberty, give them an educational book and offer to discuss it with them. Start it with them—see how things go. If they accept the interaction, continue. If they aren't that interested, don't force it. Let them continue at their own pace. This communicates belief that they can figure it out and you respect their level of development.

Internet and Video Games

When it comes to the internet and video games, screen time should be restricted before they enter elementary school. And once they start, we should strictly manage when and how much screen time they have, according to current brain development data. As they enter upper elementary and adolescence, we can give them increasing freedom to manage their time, including screen time—in general, we want to create greater opportunities for them to practice making decisions about their lives.

Again, bring this topic into your cultural context of light and heat. Alert your kids to benefits and dangers. Help them understand the power of screen activities. Put filters on home computers.

Other general management guidelines are:
4. Keep computers in "public" areas.
5. Enforce time limits for being online.

As your kids grow, don't be afraid to gradually hand over the reins; this communicates belief and trust in them as well as offering opportunities for failure. Remember the section in Chapter 10 on failure and how it provides essential opportunities for practice and greater learning. More significantly, we parents also need to have many chances to practice how we respond to and deal with mistakes and failures. This demonstrates our true character and values in the only ways that our children will deeply believe. It authenticates whether or not we are truly growth-centered.

Drugs and Alcohol

With a growth-centered culture, more things are brought into the light and warmth of true love. Less is kept in the dark, where it produces fear, shame and stress. Addictive and abusive drug and alcohol use are the result of keeping thoughts, feelings, and even ourselves isolated from love. Having conversations and a growing culture of relational comfort fortifies our family members against harmful, toxic practices.

Don't make the discussion taboo, creating negative perceptions. Equip your children with facts to inform and protect them. The main dangers to be aware of are isolation and busyness—both tend to disconnect us from each other. Depending on the amount of time your family has been growth centered, generating environments, it's possible to find comfort in substances and activities rather than people. This means we leaders (parents) need to keep this on our dashboard. We've got to be aware of the emotional climate of our loved ones. What are they feeling and how are they dealing with things? What are we feeling and how are we dealing? It begins with us. We will get more into this later in this chapter, where I share some personal growth tools.

Passing on Beliefs and Values

Think about your children as adults. How do you hope they'll handle their time, money, and energy? How do you want them to manage conflict? What is the trajectory you want for their relationships?

Rather than blindly hope for the best, we need to distinguish our notional values from our real values. Real values come from core beliefs that drive our daily decisions and activities. These values and beliefs are the truths governing our world.

Much of the time, the values are defaults we may not be aware of, based on either love or fear. Is our default deep affection, fondness, tenderness, warmth, intimacy, attachment, endearment? Or is it a feeling of unease, apprehension, or concern that diminishes creative power resulting in conformity? As parents, we want to pass on beliefs and values supporting our children's development to being liberated leaders, not blind or anxious followers.

Core Beliefs

I want my core beliefs and values to effectively encourage my family members to grow in the Seven Levels of Leadership (see the chart at https://www.valuescentre.com/mapping-values/barrett-model/leadership-consciousness). We get into trouble when our values cause us to neglect lower levels while pursuing higher ones. To avoid this, it helps to simply understand that there is a progression—each level appropriately supports the ones above it. Once we understand this, we want to create new experiences through our choices, actions, efforts, and perseverance. Here's a brief description of the various levels of consciousness we want all family members to transit.

Levels 1-3 are controlled by insecurity. It's not that the higher levels don't have insecurity, but they are not controlled by it. Patterns of choice and behavior are driven by not having or being enough—money, protection, love, care, acceptance, belonging, power, authority, status. Overcoming these fundamental challenges with healthy, appropriate support through initiative, trial and error, and loved ones will help us prepare for the critical transition through Level 4: transformation.

Level 4 is where we become more aware of our default fears and confront fear-based childhood beliefs to manage, master, or release them.

As we break free from the control of negative, instinctual beliefs, we experience the transformation ushering us into living and leading higher motivations; this is what frees us to be true to who we really are. We submit to the yearning to find meaning through causes and purposes that come from our hearts, rather than just what others direct. We pursue fulfillment, giving our unique gift and exploring our creative potential.

Level 5 is where our minds and hearts unite and we're able to find our highest purpose. We establish our life's vision and mission, tapping into our deepest passion and creativity.

Level 6 is living in this new awareness and emotional maturity. Collaborating with others, we make a bigger difference in whatever we're doing.

Level 7 is when making a real difference becomes a way of life. Our impact, influence, and intentionality empower us to leave a legacy of love and benevolence at home and work.

"A belief is not merely an idea that the mind possesses. It is an idea that possesses the mind." —Robert Oxton Bolton

What beliefs do you want possessing your mind? What values and priorities will foster healthy growth and development?

Not all of these life determiners are equal, meaning there may be inner life codes we operate under that are not helping us and our family members mature. We need to grow our understanding of our interiors to decide what will center us for effective maturation.

Part Three Summary

Remember that practice is the key to increase strength, flexibility and mobility. This is true with physical exercise and it is also true for our spiritual emotional fitness.

When it comes to the issue of what we become, our consistent activities are the most potent. The more often we repeat them, the greater the impact on our being. A gardener regularly tends to her garden to create a place of order, beauty, and health. She landscapes, works the soil, determines the best locations for the benefit of each plant as well as the overall environment. This is a great simile for raising a family, the gardeners being the members and the garden being the environment of relationships. This means the parents are also training and developing young gardeners who eventually create and cultivate their own gardens.

To do this work effectively, we must grow our emotional fitness to overcome the challenges involved—rejection, loneliness, guilt, rumination, trauma, failure, and low self-esteem. We have our kids for eighteen years, give or take a few; hopefully we have our spouses for decades. This means we've got to persevere, to last. The interior workouts given in this chapter develop deeper and broader perspectives to deal with emotional injuries and pain in healing ways. This is what grounds us to our sources of energy to keep us going with faith, hope, and love.

Our daily practices and behaviors in the home, with each other and on our own, center us. When they incorporate activities that foster emotional, relational, and spiritual health, our families are centered on growth. We see our spouse, our kids, and even ourselves become more courageous, compassionate, creative, adaptable, and successful in managing and leading changes. If our consistent actions do not prioritize the interior life, we experience disintegration. We may find success in our work, but fail at home. Jesus Christ asked the question, "What good will it be for someone to gain the whole world, yet forfeit their soul?" That is, lose connectedness to what is most meaningful— loved ones. Cultivate what matters most and avoid inferior centers. Center on growth and see your family thrive!

Postface: Sustainable Growth

I want to leave you with one last thought about growth. Growth by itself is not the be-all end-all. Growth has to be healthy and sustainable. Cancer is growth but not the kind we want; it's not sustainable; it diminishes and kills. Maturation must be in harmony within a system. Ideal growth is infinitely sustainable—eternal!

Healthy, sustainable growth is an indicator of true love. When we are truly loving over sustained periods of time, when we are consistent and committed in thought and actions to loving God, others, and ourselves, we are growth centered. But if our values and behaviors do not reflect authentic love, we end up centering on things that prevent ongoing growth and development. We are not be able to help others reach their highest potentials (physically, spiritually, emotionally, cognitively, professionally, relationally), especially the ones we love most and want to do the most good for.

Sustainable growth is aligning with what matters most in the long run, overcoming the struggles to do so within oneself, dysfunctional relationships, and stunting environments. Sustainable growth redeems those challenges with greater communication and collaboration as we improve our ethics with long-term perspectives. With greater health, we achieve fulfillment for all—first and foremost at home, then work and beyond.

To the sustainable renewal of all people by being growth centered.

Appendix

Tools to Grow Your Interior Life

This section provides some tools to engage the intangibles that many people miss, do not prioritize enough, and/or do not apply widely enough to support their growth and development. Dealing with these hidden things involves life work necessary to clarify what's going on underneath the surface. Over time, exploring the things that drive our daily default decisions shapes and directs us. Hopefully, these subsurface motivations drive us toward becoming who we really are; but more often than not, they lessen our potential and distract us from what we really want—stronger, healthier bodies, souls, and relationships. But this work empowers us to fulfill our needs and make continual progress—first at home, where it's most meaningful and needed, then beyond. It's what helps us meet transcendent needs to help others achieve their highest potentials.

Tool #1: A.I.R.

First things first: we've got to breathe A.I.R. (Awareness, Identify, Reflect). Regularly exercising this skill empowers you to abide in empathy to manage emotional reactivity.[42]

Think about the last time something happened that caused you to be anger, sadness, or fear. Then breathe, reflect, and answer the following questions:

1. What did you see, hear, observe? (Sensory data)
2. How did you interpret the data? (Thoughts)
3. What feelings did the interpretation generate? (Emotions)
4. What do you want for yourself? For the other person? For both of you? (Wants)
5. What do you want to do differently? (Actions)

As you know, air quality is not the same for all locations. If you want clean air, you need to get away from pollution. This is essential to this exercise. Get somewhere that refreshes your mind—somewhere with beauty, somewhere in nature, a place that inspires you. This could be a relationship or a physical location. It could be an activity.

---

[42] "Introducing You to Yourself", Aphesis Group, 2011, Week 19.

Once you've arrived somewhere with better "air," now go through the A.I.R. process. It can take as much time as you want; just make sure you do it again before too much passes—no more than a day or two. The challenge is to make it regular. Just remember what you're doing—breathing. Not getting oxygen to parts of your body is damaging. You may not feel it immediately, but just like with anything else, waiting too long will make repairs costly or even impossible—think amputation. But even then, restoration can occur if we keep up oxygenating practices over extended time. Given brain plasticity, redemption and renewal are entirely possible.

Tool #2: The Dissociation Cycle

The dissociation cycle is an important mechanism—it involves our triggers and responses to pain, and the outcomes that arise in response. It actually starts with our desire to be free from pain. There's nothing inherently wrong with pain; it is simply how our body communicates to some form of healing or comfort is in order.

Over time, we develop default decisions on dealing with pain. This is where trust in the early years is very formative, because under normal circumstances, the healthiest form of relief and comfort is people with whom we have relationships. However, if our trust is broken, our desire to be free from pain becomes confused and unhealthy. We're driven toward ineffective, short-term, enslaving ways to get rid of the pain because the healthy alternative has been eliminated.

This chaotic drive dissociates us from the reality of emotional pain-finding deliverance. This separates our souls from our will, mind, and body. It is often so radical that we're not even aware of it. We develop non-relational ways to find comfort. Our actions and behaviors may give temporary relief, but just cause more emotional pain for ourselves and others, which kicks off the cycle again.

We need to recognize our dysfunctional response to get rid of our pain and find a new way of connecting with someone who is emotionally and relationally healthy. This needs to be a person with whom you can share deeply, who is strongly committed to the wellness of your soul, mind, and body. This person will help you find association with reality to act in ways restoring rest, peace, emotional health, and freedom.

So, to get out of the cycle, we must find a different response to free ourselves from pain and fear. Try thinking about the following:

- For starters, what actions and temporary reliefs/pleasures seem to cause more emotional pain for you (fear, shame, loneliness, guilt, anxiety)?
- What might be the narrative or perspective that drives those actions? ("No one cares anyway...I'll always be alone...that's how it is and nothing's going to change...talking about it won't change anything...people never change.")
- What causes your desire to be free from pain to become evil (chaotic/confused)?

Once you find this clarity, work toward selecting your new response to pain. In addition to healthy, gracious people, we can't overlook God.

Why God? As Creator, He knows and understands how we are wired and what we need to function at our best. As a good, heavenly Father, He wants our spirit to be free and healthy, living life with abundant courage, patience, security, freedom, and joy. As a redeeming God, He has the power to work all things toward our good as we believe and take steps to change our lives. As a wise counselor, He knows the depths of our soul, our needs, and the most effective, empowering ways to comfort our pain to strengthen us to grow and move forward.

Bottom line: We need healthy relationships to help us break free from these cycles. They are rooted in unhealthy relationships, where we learned un-relational ways to find comfort and security. So then, solutions will be found in relational ways, not more isolation. Being mindful isn't easy; it's quite uncomfortable. But with time and practice, it can be a healthy, regular activity that will develop greater strength, flexibility, and resilience.

Tool #3: The Lord's Prayer
Forgiveness is Freedom

This ancient prayer expresses what matters most for a healthy family. When a man and woman love and commit to each other, become "one flesh" for life, they lay the foundation for a family. Being one flesh creates an environment of trust, security, and intimacy freeing each other to grow their love, raise the next generation, preparing them to raise another.

The family is supposed to be the place for the next generation to grow and learn about life, what is most important. It should also develop leadership so the children are able to transition into adulthood with character and competence. When this environment is healthy, it helps children grow the capacity and ability to make good decisions.

Over many generations, it is common for families to be compromised by outdated, limiting rules, beliefs, values, and habits. Relationships disintegrate when conflict was poorly handled, and the most important parts of being human are forgotten or neglected.

The Lord's Prayer can be a tool to help us regain a more holistic priority for our homes. It identifies the things that grow inner life dynamics that can renew our families. Prayer is actually intended to be breathing (A.I.R.) with God; it's a different response to fear and pain. And in this prayer, Jesus gave a template of elements that teach us about a spiritual, emotionally healthy family.

Knowing people, and their common inner life challenges, Jesus began with, "'Our Father in heaven…" addressing God as Father, a father of a family that prioritizes a healthy atmosphere of relationships (heaven).

With "…hallowed be your name…" Jesus was saying Father God's priority set Him apart. His authority and care centering on relationships made Him unique from other gods and rulers.

"…your kingdom come, your will be done, on earth as it is in heaven." Jesus expressed His desire for the Father's priority to be a reality in everyday moments. And for this to happen, Jesus asked, "Give us today our daily bread. And forgive us our debts, as we also have forgiven our debtors," that is, for the daily provision of forgiveness, involving forgiving others and being forgiven.

"And lead us not into temptation, but deliver us from the evil one." Regularly forgiving and being forgiven results in freedom from the snags of temptations and lies that devastate us and our families—i.e., the myths of scarcity which drive us toward willful blindness. When we are not controlled by these destructive forces, our relationships can thrive.

Tool #4: Crucial Conversations

If we spend enough time with another person, we experience situations where we will need to have difficult conversations. Whether or not it happens depends on our openness to tension and engaging fear. How well it happens depends on our level of emotional health and maturity, as well as previous opportunities to learn and practice this skill.

"Mastering crucial conversations kick-starts your career, strengthens your relationships, improves your health."[43] This is becoming more and more recognized in the workplace, but it needs to be applied even more at home. If we want to be effective parents, we must master these kinds of conversations. Just think how much better everyone in a family will handle the teenage years and how much less damage will occur if parents and youth communicate well in tough moments. Having crucial conversations at home helps every member be better prepared for making positive impact and change in the world. Check out their Youtube channel (https://www.youtube.com/vitalsmarts).

Patterson et al define crucial conversations with the following elements:[44] high stakes, strong differences, and strong emotions. When these three things show up, the following are likely to follow: silence and/or violence caused by our fight/flight response, intensity caused by

---

[43] Ibid, p.9.

[44] *Crucial Conversations: Tools for Talking When Stakes are High*, by Kerry Patterson, Joseph Grenny, Ron McMillan, and Al Switzler.

lack of emotional health/intelligence, exacerbated by busyness and prioritizing productivity over relationships.

When these situations arise, we need to work at identifying and remembering the goal that matters most—shared meaning with each other. We want this pool to be as deep and clear as possible; this fosters meaningful trust and intimacy. And this encourages learning and creates openness to change.

For crucial conversations to be authentic and sincere, they cannot be formulaic. They need to flow from a heart that is not driven, but rather believing and humble. The key element will be our stories. This means our souls play a crucial role, as they are responsible for making meaning. Go back to Chapter 7 if you need to refresh what our souls need to thrive. Better yet, pick up a copy of Ortberg's *Soul Keeping*.

The challenges of these conversations are numerous. We need to slow down enough to get deeper. We need consistent awareness of our stories. We need courage to choose a different story and commitment to change it. It's a whole other level of thought to develop stories that reflect what is going on (the bigger picture), as well as to engage and transform the ones embedded from our youth and/or negative experiences.

We may need to modify our cause and effect beliefs. Conflict will not drive us apart. We may need to change our perceptions of our roles and relationships—"I'm not a victim and this relationship does not have to have a winner and loser." Everyone in this home can learn that pain-producing problems are not always bad, quick fixes should not be the norm, and we can work together to find long-term solutions. Ultimately, our new stories should center on love that drives out fear of loss.

When we get better and better at crucial conversations, we look forward to greater freedom from immature, incomplete, inaccurate, impotent stories. When we master them rather than having them master us—or better yet, when God's story of love and liberty masters us—we are empowered to write the ending with grace and truth. We will be 100% honest and 100% respectful.

This is what's needed to reconcile tense situations and chronic dysfunction. With greater clarity from healthier perspectives, we are able to make changes that move us toward growth of shared meaning with another rather than being led astray to behave as disparate, isolated individuals. Effectively managing these situations moves us toward being one flesh to foster the growth environment we need.

Tool #5: The Comfort Circle

This next tool, the Comfort Circle[45], comes from Milan and Kay Yerkovich, two amazing people who exemplify living life centered on growth. This tool helps us increase our self-awareness to acknowledge what emotions overwhelm during stress and tension. Here is an infographic (https://www.relationship180.com/resources/). This process is best done with someone you trust, but it is also a good self-reflection tool. The Yerkoviches have created a great list of 'feeling' words'[46] to help. Take a moment to check it out.

As you clarify your feelings and the stories driving them, explore your needs and wants. The difficulty here is getting past certain beliefs and rules about life acting as gatekeepers. They might've been set up early on as a protective default, but after closer, thoughtful examination, you may want to fire them. They may be keeping you from successfully overcoming the challenges of growing intimacy, generativity, and integrity.

By slowing down, we are listened to, whether by another or ourselves, and the reality of our emotions is validated. "Yes, I'm really hurt and angry right now, and what that person said or did *was* hurtful." Slow down some more so the inner dialogue continues, "Was it intentional? What's going on inside of them right now? What do I want

---

[45] **Milan and Kay Yerkovich**, https://www.howwelove.com/blog/tag/comfort-circle/

[46] Ibid, https://s3.amazonaws.com/hwl-prod-assets/uploads/2012/05/16030007/SoulWordList.pdf

for myself? My loved one? Our relationship?" Here, we may run into old narratives that derail our dialogue. However, if we practice slowing down, creating the time for this kind of reflection, we're more apt to exercise crucial evaluations and modifications to our thoughts, beliefs, and values that move us forward. As we slow the process and add logic and analysis, we keep our left-brain engaged so that the emotional side of ourselves does not dominate. Recall and meditate on the love others have for you. Create time and space to be inspired and rejuvenated. But the biggest thing is the practice of slowing down, getting vulnerable, and putting in effort to be mindful about the bigger picture.

Resolution comes as we ask ourselves, "What do I need to help me deal with this better?" Perhaps sharing deeply with another will do it. Or, solitude may be what's needed. It may be helpful to do slow rhythmic breathing. Perhaps asking God to help in this place of pain. Or go for a walk or hit the gym. To help your brain see thoughts in black and white, write them in a journal. Then, read your entries aloud and evaluate your thoughts with yourself or another. This helps your brain process in a different manner, which helps your mind increase perspective. Resolve may take time; it can't be rushed. Substantial shift occurs as we create time to slow down and increase our attention, intention, and repetition of interior life development in relation with another. Power is found in commitment to practice.

This kind of comfort is radically different from the quick, easy fixes common and normative in our society. But deep, relational comfort is what liberates us from dissociative behaviors and cycles. And the healthier the people we engage in this, the more freedom, healing, and empowerment we will experience.

Tool #6: Centrality of Forward-Moving Relationships

This last tool provides a good overall picture of dynamic elements in a growth-centered family. In order for our relationships to thrive. We need these four trust-building elements. They help us get to know each other more deeply. They empower us to be truly present and learn how to be better—to know and lead ourselves so we can also positively influence the other. With all four, our relationships will enable and encourage all members to grow and mature.

This first is a key foundation: empathy before consequences. Empathy is the source of connection. When we truly put ourselves in the shoes of another, we slow down to be with them, physically, mentally, and emotionally, and we're able to cultivate an environment of trust. For balanced, healthy empathy, we need to be able to understand and feel the other person's thoughts and feelings, but also have clear boundaries for our own. We don't get lost in the other person; that would not move the relationship, or each other, forward. So, I want to reemphasize the primary importance of regularly working on ourselves. We've got to have our own oxygen masks on before being any real support for another.

Secondly, we need to share our thoughts with each other. Being transparent is half of this activity. It's important to reveal our thoughts and feelings so the other can know us. Expecting others to read our minds is immature and ineffective in building trust. The other half of this activity is being safe. This means withholding judgment and quick interpretations of the facts—being curious and staying open longer to hear and understand what the other is trying to communicate. This means we must grow how we share our thoughts, which means we need to grow the perspective from where they come. If we openly share thoughts that shut down the other, we won't be moving anyone forward.

Thirdly, we need to recognize that responsibilities for healthy relationships are shared. We only move forward when both members own what helps the relationship thrive. When problems occur, both parties take on what is appropriate for their age to work toward solutions.

Lastly, we must foster a culture of respect. Keeping calm and curious prevents heated, tense moments from becoming shouting matches, sarcastic attacks, or silent killers. Rather than slip into avoidance or aggression, we want to be honest and respectful, expressing the value and worth of each. We don't want to make others feel inferior, but rather hold them up as one worthy of honor and able to hear the truth. Again, to achieve this, parents must lead the way with bold work, developing our interiors. It is our personal, emotional, and even spiritual maturity which creates the safe space for all this to happen.

Bibliography

Alan Watkins, *4D Leadership: Competitive Advantage Through Vertical Leadership Development,* Kogan Pages, London 1st Edition, 2015.

Alpha International, The Parenting Children's Course, London (2011).

Aphesis Group, *Introducing You to Yourself*, 2011.

The Holy Bible, New International Version. Grand Rapids: Zondervan House, 1984.

Bruce Lipton, *Biology of Belief,* Sounds True Inc; Edition (2007-01-17)

Edwin Catmull and Amy Wallace, *Creativity Inc.,* Random House, New York City, NY; 1 edition (April 8, 2014).

Gary Chapman, *The 5 Love Languages: The Secret to Love That Lasts*, Northfields Publishing, Chicago, IL, 2010.

Guy Winch, *Emotional Firs Aid,* Penguin Random House, New York City, NY, 2013.

Hal Runkel, *Scream-free Parenting,* Penguin Random House, New York City, NY, 2007.

Jim Collins and Jerry Porras, *Built to Last: Successful Habits of Visionary Companies*, HarperCollins Publishers, New York City, NY, 2011.

John Ortberg and Tommy Cresswell, *Soul Keeping,* Grand Rapids: Zondervan House, 2014.

Joseph Grenney, Kerry Patterson, Ron McMillan, Al Switzler, *Crucial Conversations,* Brilliance Audio; 2nd Updated ed. edition *(August 1, 2013).*

Lynne Twist and Cynthia Barrett, *Soul of Money,* Audible Studios, 2013.

Margaret Heffernan, *Willful Blindness,* Audible Studios, 2011.

Marilyn Mandala Schlitz, Cassandra Vieten, Tina Amorok, *Living Deeply: The Art and Science of Transformation in Everyday Life*, New Harbinger Publications, Oakland, CA, 2008.

Milan and Kay Yerkovich, *How We Love,* WaterBrook, Colorado Springs, CO; Later Printing edition, 2008.

Thomas Phelan and Paul Costanzo, *1-2-3 Magic,* Tantor Audio, Old Saybrook, CT, 2016.

Verne Harnish and Spencer Cannon, *Scaling Up,* Gazelles Inc., San Diego, CA, 2014.

Vishen Lakiani, *The Code of the Extraordinary Mind,* Rodale Books (1858), Emmaus, PA, 2016.

Made in the USA
San Bernardino, CA
15 December 2017